LIVING ON THE EDG

CONTENTS

First published in the United Kingdom by Arc Publishing and Print 2018

ISBN: 978-1-906722-56-2

MAP OF UPPER HALLAM

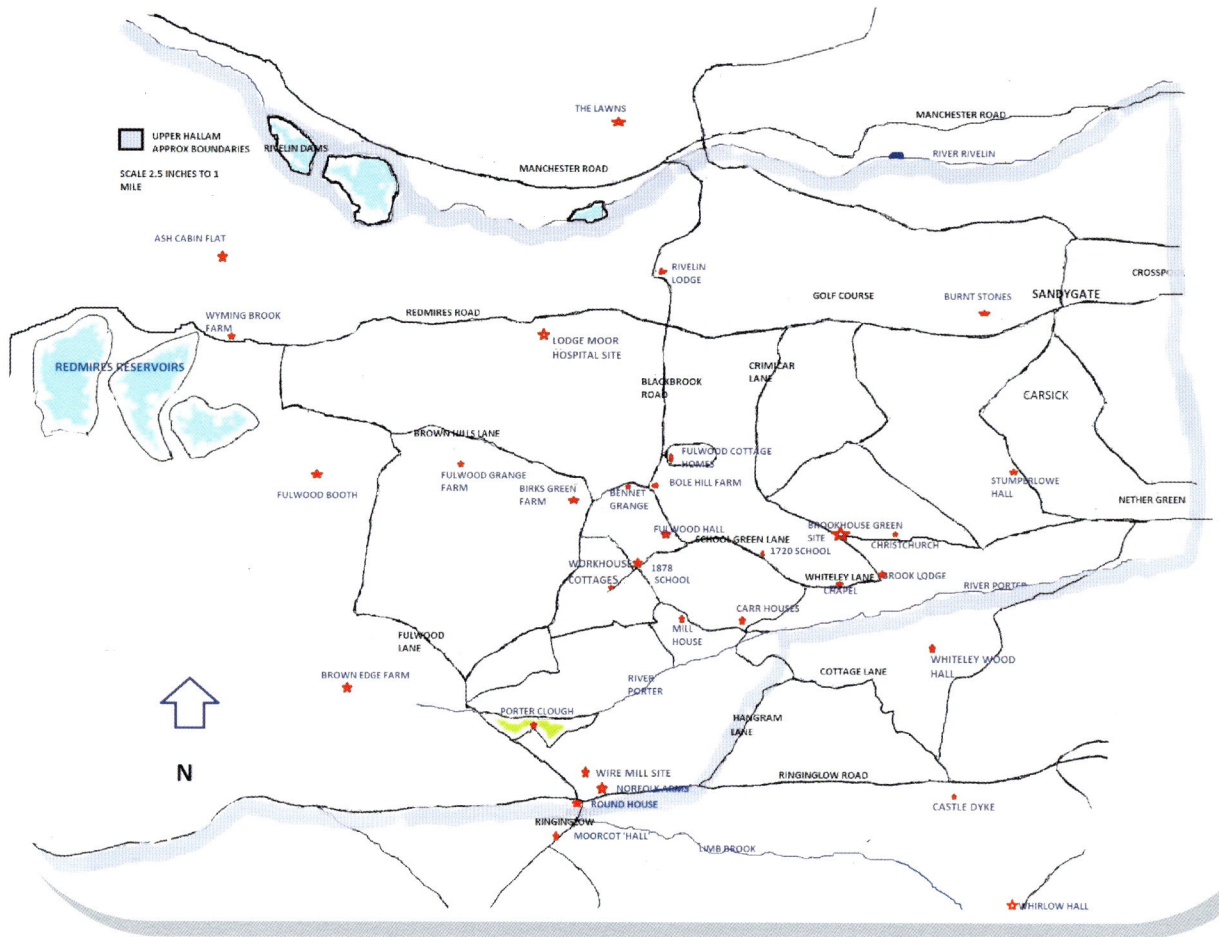

Fig 1

The above diagram shows most of the Township of Upper Hallam—one of the six such townships that made up Sheffield. The township extends further west as far as Stanedge Pole. The places marked with a red star are those mentioned in this book

INTRODUCTION

Please allow me to introduce myself. I'm a man of wealth and taste. Well, quite an exaggeration in both cases, but I grew up in the Rolling Stones era and the wildness and refusal to accept convention that attracted me to their music finds an echo in the area in Fulwood where I have lived for over 30 years now.

I am neither an historian nor an academic. I suppose I am just a magpie, picking up shiny pieces of information and seeing what I can do with them. The result is this collection of people and places with a connection to the far South-South-West of Sheffield within a mile or two of my home. It does not pretend to be comprehensive. There are many interesting places, people and stories that have been omitted, not because I think they are in any way inferior to those I have included, but because I am a magpie and I have my own pecking order.

Most of the information I have used comes from some excellent books I have read. In particular I would recommend the many books by David Hey on Sheffield and South Yorkshire and Muriel Hall's two books, 'Mayfield Valley' (now out of print and hard to obtain but available in the Local Studies Library in Sheffield) and 'More of Mayfield Valley with Old Fulwood' which is more readily available on that site beginning with 'A'. There are also several books I have listed under sources that I have much enjoyed reading. These are the books that introduced me to the interest and variety of this area and took me to some fascinating places, too numerous to mention in full.

The staff at the Local Studies Library and Sheffield Archives have all been unfailingly helpful and deserve a medal for their efforts in retrieving so many ancient documents from their vaults for me. The area that I live in is right at the far SSW edge of Sheffield. Snow seems to like it here and at least one day a year usually sees you snowed in. It is amazing though how many manage to make it on foot all the way out to 'The Three Merry Lads' despite the blizzard conditions on those days. This photograph shows exactly how wild it can be up here. The snow is sometimes whipped up from the fields and it can feel more like the Antarctic than South Yorkshire.

Fig 2 View from near Fullwood Hall March 2018

Derbyshire is a stone's throw away. It was even closer at one time. Beauchief Abbey was then in Derbyshire. This means we are not only on the far edge of Sheffield, but we are also on the far edge of Yorkshire here.

It seems it was always like that. We were on the boundary of the Brigantes' territory in the pre-Roman days, and, for a while this area was on the Roman frontier before the Romans overwhelmed the Brigantes and the frontier moved further north. After the Romans we became a buffer zone between Northumbria and Mercia where the Limb Brook was the actual boundary.

Even in matters of religion we were on the edge. Non-Conformists settled and became influential here. This was the closest they were allowed to come to Sheffield at the time.

Maybe there is something in the water here. Certainly there is plenty of it. The Mayfield and Porter Brooks, the Limb valley and the Rivelin are all close by and have attracted people here for thousands of years. Some of their stories fill these pages. There is even a spa somewhere, if you can find it!

The odd sketch is mine as are the photographs.

The people mentioned in this book come from all periods of history and levels of society. Some were generous and public spirited, some were dissolute, a couple died tragically, another was obsessed with the properties of water. One would not be out of place as a pantomime villain and another managed to put his head back on after being decapitated. You could say that they constitute a fairly normal cross-section of everyday Fulwood folk and the landscape they inhabit. Even Robin Hood makes a brief appearance.
.

I hope this birds-eye view of the area stimulates your interest to find, or look again, at some of the places here. There are plenty of easily accessible footpaths, for the reasonably fit, shown marked on the Ordnance Survey map and many good walks in this area are suggested on websites.

I have tried to give credit to the sources I have used in the narrative. The list of sources includes all the books and websites I have enjoyed while putting together this meandering ramble. These sources include much further information on various important aspects of this region including the use and growth of water power and the production of local cutlery, Phoebe Silcock, the church at Fulwood, and extensive quarrying are all important in the development of this region and are dealt with in the books and websites I have mentioned. The petition, Ivor Gatty's article, John Fox's will and one or two other deeds and documents, are based on my transcriptions from originals in Sheffield archives. Any errors, misunderstandings, or omissions I put down to my bird brain.

CHAPTER 1

<u>EARLY HUNTERS AT WHIRLOW</u>

Whirlow Hall Farm has been popular for a very long time as a place to take our children and grandchildren. What most of us who have wandered around the farm with junior companions over the years do not realize is that we have been continuing a tradition that goes back thousands of years.

After the last ice age (roughly 10,000 years ago) vegetation and wildlife gradually returned to this region to replace what were tundra conditions . Man soon followed in pursuit of food. Mesolithic people were nomads, presumably making a temporary camp while they hunted around Whirlow. We just go there to look at the animals or to buy food and then shelter in the café with its crook beams. The whole place has a sense of age.

The recent excavation at Whirlow farm has discovered some of the Mesolithic hunters' stone tools (lithics), both in nearby fields and also in trenches dug at the site. The number found is relatively small but the following is a direct quotation from the ARS Ltd Report no 297/54. dated April 2017 The full report is on the excellent Archaeological Research Services Ltd website http://archaeologicalresearchservices.com/projects/whirlow-hall-farm. Regular updates can be found at http://www.thetimetravellers.org.uk/.

'Discussion

5.51 The area around Whirlow Hall Farm has evidently formed a focus for Mesolithic activity, as evidenced by the Mesolithic material recovered by a fieldwalking survey as well as by the finds from these excavations. The main Mesolithic lithic scatters identified by the fieldwalking included two fields to the north-west of the excavation trench on rising ground close to the eastern lip of the Limb Valley. The valley provides a natural routeway for both animals and humans and gives access from the head of the Sheaf Valley on to the high moorlands above. Trench 1 was located in a similar setting although in this case it is set back from the edge of the valley side by approximately 140 metres. By being located over the lip of the eastern valley side groups would have been sheltered from the prevailing westerly winds whilst also being strategically located to monitor and control human and animal access up and down the valley. This would have afforded many opportunities to take a variety of animals, such as red and roe deer, wild pig and so forth, as well as to trap fish in the Limb Brook and take nesting birds from the rich woodland that would have mantled much of this area. The Limb Brook itself would have provided freshwater, whilst the area chosen for the settlement-type activities evidenced by the flint assemblages would have been relatively free-draining. The abundance of foodstuffs available in this general location must have been an important draw. Animals will have been attracted to water in the Limb Brook, whilst fish, fowl and birdlife could also have been easily taken. Furthermore, the plant foods and vegetation within and above the Limb Valley could have provided important sources of food, building materials and possibly clothing.'

Fig 3 Whirlow Hall Farm as it is today

It was an attractive place then and it is now. The Mesolithic is described as the era of the hunter-gatherers. The next era, the Neolithic, was when farming encouraged people to settle in an area on a permanent or at least less temporary basis. It is hoped that some evidence of Neolithic activity, or even settlement, in the area will be found but, at the time of writing, only a little from that era has been discovered either by field walking or from the pre 2018 excavations that have taken place. There have been plenty of Iron Age and Roman period finds (of which more in the next chapter) but there is little evidence of substantial early Neolithic activity in this area to date. A large enclosure , possibly a henge, is currently (2018) being excavated and, in which, a significant amount of flint has being found . As flint is not indigenous to Sheffield this may well become significant in confirming permanent Neolithic activity here

The oldest, nearby evidence for Neolithic settlement lies in Magnesian Limestone areas such as White Peak in Derbyshire, only spreading to this area of South Yorkshire in the later Neolithic, around 3000 BC. From finds it seems that settlement spread along the Rivelin, Porter Limb and Sheaf river valleys towards what is now Sheffield passing through Fulwood and the surrounding area on the way.

When pulling down a wall at Redmires, some Neolithic Rock Art, in the form of cup marks, was found on one of the stones, (which is now in Weston Park Museum.) It is likely that there are as yet undiscovered finds and even possible settlements. It is sometimes said that the number of finds for any period are in direct correlation to the number of archaeologists looking for them. Maybe that will prove to be the case here, now that Whirlow Hall Farm is attracting such archaeological interest.

A Neolithic axe and flint knife have been found on the way to Ringinglow, near the farm forming the Alpaca centre just off Fulwood Lane, There have also been other individual finds in the region. So far though, nothing has been discovered indicative of permanent settlement so characteristic of the transition from the Mesolithic lifestyle, following the animal herds, to the more settled Neolithic way of life, in which growing crops and raising animals became much more established and permanent.

The next era, according to traditional divisions, was the Bronze age, dating from around 2,200BC to 800BC. There are many barrows and grave goods from this era , which is a good indication that the local area was being permanently inhabited by then. The pottery bowls illustrated overleaf show a degree of sophistication and the Rock Art in Ecclesall Woods (also illustrated) are a significant development on the basic cup and ring marks more typical of the earlier Neolithic period.

The Bronze Age began in around 2,200 BC (although all such ages are artificial as changes seem to have come gradually over centuries rather than at any specific time). Some wonderful pottery urns have been discovered and are on display at Weston Park Museum. One of the largest and most impressive was found in Crookes in which a smaller urn was also found together with human cremated remains, a dagger burnt in the cremation, a small bowl and an arrowhead. They are proudly displayed at Weston Park museum. Do go and visit if you can

Fig 4 The two urns and bowl among the items found at Crookes in Weston Park Museum

Hidden in Ecclesall woods is a small piece of probable Bronze Age rock art, believed to have been created between 2000 and 1000BC. It is a comparatively recent discovery.

The site is not terribly easy to find but the photograph shows more complex symbols of rock art than the earlier, Neolithic, cup and ring marks Maybe it is a local map. Who knows?

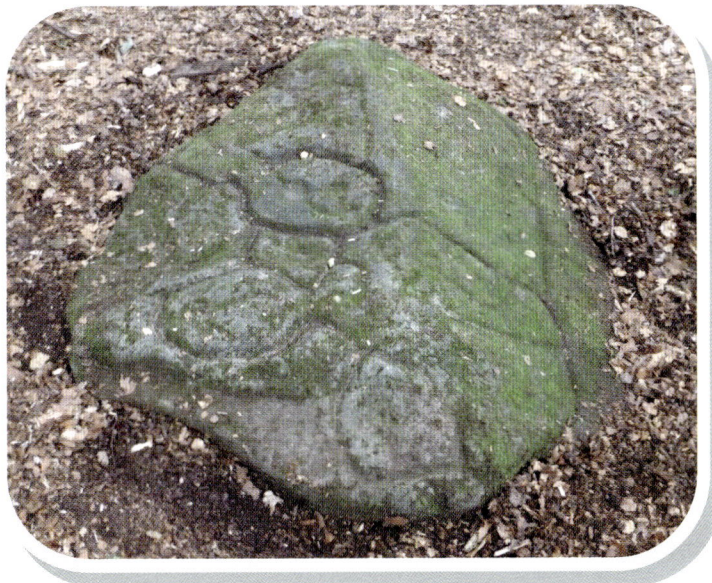

Fig 5 Bronze Age Rock Art from Ecclesall Woods

CHAPTER 2

SON OF ALBANUS AND THE RIVELIN VALLEY

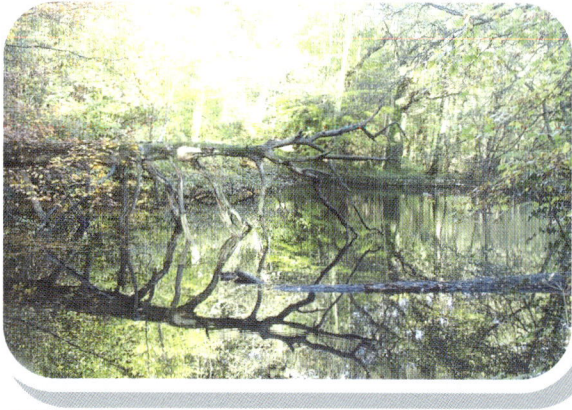

Fig 6 Reflections on the Rivelin

According to the Rev Joseph Hunter in chapter 2 of his 1819 work 'Hallamshire. The History and Topography of the Parish of Sheffield 'Edward Nichols was ploughing a piece of common land called 'the Lawns' on the Stannington side of the Rivelin Valley in April 1761,when, near a large stone, he discovered two thin copper plates each measuring about 6"x 5". They contained Latin inscriptions. When translated these were found to state that, in AD 124, a member of the Germanic Sunici tribe (from modern day East Belgium, Southern Netherlands and the German area around Cologne, a veteran auxiliary foot soldier in the 1st cohort of the Sunici of the Roman Imperial Army) was granted Roman Citizenship by the then Emperor, Hadrian. There was nothing unusual in this. After serving on campaign for 25 years it was Roman Imperial policy to grant citizenship to their soldiers often together with land in the conquered territory in which those soldiers were serving as a means of Romanizing the local population, or as Hunter pictures it:-

'[the veterans] *settle themselves in a small colony on the banks of the Riveling (sic) allured perhaps by the representations of some petty Cartismandua attached to her native soil and woodland stream, and who made a settlement in that place the price of her charms to the Roman veteran'*

Whether or not the son of Albanus gave his address as The Lawns, Rivelin Valley is open to debate. Wherever he lived, his settlement has not been found, although the farm called 'The Lawns' still remains. In his book 'The Roman Diploma of AD 124' Michael Dyson narrows down the find spot to a place between The Lawns and Rails farm. He says the finder, a farmer and cutlery manufacturer, lived at Rails farm and was clearing the land prior to ploughing. He also reports that the piece of land in which the diplomas were found was known as King's Park or Penny piece. How and why the copper plates came to be there is a mystery but it is more likely than not that the veteran had left the army to settle somewhere in this region even if the place the plates were found were not actually his home.

It is possible that Albanus Junior was previously employed in the Roman enclosure at Whirlow. In around 69AD ,according to the current archaeological findings at Whirlow Hall Farm, this replaced a pre-existing Iron Age enclosure estimated to have been originally constructed sometime between 350 and 121 BC

In 2016 the foundations of a short-lived wooden Roman signal station were found on the highest ground close by. It seems the site was on a significant supply line all across the frontier that included Templeborough in the East and Brough and Baltham Gate in the West. It is likely to have been built in the recently annexed former Brigantes territory after that tribe ceased being allies of Rome in AD69. The possible signal station is believed to have continued in operation (or at least physically still present) until around 130 AD, the time our soldier was pensioned off. He may even have been chief signaller

Fig 7 How the wooden signal station at Whirlow may have appeared. It is likely to have had a surrounding wooden palisade fence and a ditch.

for all we know! Signals would have been sent to other signal towers within sight and on either side of the one at Whirlow so warnings could be sent by relay all along the frontier. The tower may have been thatched and the signals sent by smoking poles. This certainly happened elsewhere in the Empire.

The area already had several farms. There was a pre-existing hilltop enclosure (possibly used for storage of farm produce) in what is now Ecclesall Woods as well as the substantial Brigantine enclosure at Whirlow later occupied by the Romans. It may be our ex-soldier went into farming to supply the army occupying the former Brigantes territory previously led by Cartismandua (hence the reference to that name by Hunter) According to the 2016 excavation report, pottery finds indicate abandonment of the enclosure site sometime in the late 200's AD to the mid 300's AD so the Roman presence here will have long outlasted our retired veteran. Maybe his descendants still live on here. There are certainly families that can claim to have remained here for centuries. Not many of them speak Latin though.

There may also have been a more famous temporary resident. In his book 'The Ancient Suburbs of Sheffield' J Edward Vickers quotes a 1620 history by Dodsworth as follows:-

Robin Locksley, born in Bradfield parish in Hallamshire, wounded his step-father to death at plough, fled into the woods, and was relieved by his mother till he was discovered. Then he came to Clifton upon Calder, and became acquainted with Little John that kept the kine. Which said John is buried at Hathershead in Derbyshire, where he hath a fair tombstone with an inscription. Little John was Earl Huntley's son. Afterwards he joined with Much the Millar's son ……

So it wasn't just in the forest at Nottingham where Robin Hood may have had a hideout. He may have started his career as an outlaw in the woods of Fulwood and the Rivelin valley, where red deer were plentiful. He would have had to avoid the head deer-keeper employed by the Lord of the Manor as '*Master of the Game*' at the rate of £2 a year and his team of underlings. Maybe it was one of those that discovered Robin's hiding place and caused him to move further afield. What a shame that we have allowed Nottingham to claim what we might well call one of our own!

The Rivelin Valley is a fascinating place. The Normans created 3 adjoining chases stretching out for thousands of acres of moorland spreading from their castle in Sheffield. Rivelin Chase was one of them. According to David Hey, in his book 'History of the South Yorkshire Countryside' it is first mentioned in 1383 but it had been used for much longer. The folk of Fulwood and other nearby places were granted grazing and other rights such as to take herbs and there is mention of a quarry in 1268 . By the time of Henry VIII, the keeper of the game at Fulwood was Henry Wrasteler, who was paid the princely sum of a three halfpennies a day for his labours. His direct superior was Thomas Shircliffe who was then Master of the Game for the whole of Hallamshire.

On the steep climb up the cliff above the valley stood a hunting lodge that may have housed Mary Stuart overnight on excursions from her imprisonment in Sheffield. The site has excellent views over the whole valley and is still a house, although much altered from Tudor days

Fig 8 A modern day Cartismandua crossing the Rivelin

The walk from the car park near Rails Road to Malin Bridge, along the river, is full of surprises. You pass through a wild wooded valley with various surviving water features of the long-since removed, ancient wheels once driven by the channelled power of the river . You sometimes have to wade through the river itself when the water levels reach above the stepping stones. On the 1903 Ordnance survey map, in the days just before the road above the valley floor was built in 1905, there are no less than 4 sets of stepping stones marked crossing the river. Maybe our friend, the son of Albinus, waded this way with his Cartismandua.

To suggest Robin and Maid Marion walked here may be stretching the bounds of possibility rather far, but anyway hang on to your valuables if you ever see a shadowy figure dressed in green in the woods. This may even be his chair......

Fig 9
Modern sculpture by the Rivelin

CHAPTER 3

<u>EARL WALTHEOF AND HIS AULA</u>

Earl Waltheof was a prominent Saxon nobleman. According to the Domesday book, he had a hall (or aula as it was called) in Hallun. This was the area that we now call Hallam. As to his hall though, no-one knows where it was, or is, so I am not going to even begin to speculate. It seems as though it had been an important place at one time but by 1086 it was no more. The local historian J Addy placed the village of Hallam in an area towards the top of Slayleigh Lane just below the Long Causeway.

Waltheof was born in around 1050 the younger son of the Dane Siward ,Earl of Northumbria, the Siward who led the army against Macbeth in Shakespeare's play. His Mother was Aelfflaed, and what a shame it is that name has dropped out of use. She was the granddaughter of Uhtred a previous Earl of Northumbria. As a much younger second son he would not have expected to inherit any family titles so it is likely he was educated for a monastic life. This changed in 1055 when his brother Siward was killed in battle in Scotland. Waltheof was much too young to inherit the Earldom and a Godwinson was appointed as the new Earl of Northumberland.

Fig 10
Waltheof at Crowland
Abbey

In 1065 Waltheof was old enough to receive an Earldom in his own right and he was granted Northamptonshire and Huntingdonshire. The old order changed somewhat in the following year and after submitting to William the Conqueror he was allowed to keep his titles and attended William's court for two years. He returned North just in time to join up with the Norseman Sweyn's 1069 invasion.. Waltheof, and a claimant to the throne, Edgar Aethling, both took part in the Sweyn armies' attack on York but the Danish fleet sailed back home in 1070 leaving Waltheof having to submit to William yet again.

Rather oddly given the vehemence of William's reaction to the invasion that led to what is known as 'the Harrying of the North',William not only gave Waltheof his Earldoms back including Northumberland, and later made him Earl of Northampton, but also allowed or encouraged him to marry William's own niece, Judith of Lens, in 1070. The marriage produced three children. One daughter married David the King of Scotland.

Despite any religious training Waltheof may have received he was quite prepared to continue a long running feud of both his and his wife's family that had been going on since at least his mother's great grandfather's time. The antagonistic family was led by Carl, son of Thurebrand. There had been several generations of murder between these families and Waltheof obviously thought it was his turn to get involved. In 1074, Hunter reports that Waltheof's retainers murdered Carl's two eldest sons 'while they were carousing at Settrington in the Yorkshire Wolds'.

In 1075 the Earl's Revolt against William broke out in the North. Historians and contemporaries are divided as to what part, if any, that Waltheof may have had in this rebellion. It has been alleged that Judith betrayed her husband although it seems that she, herself, had a number of enemies, one of whom , a monk, went so far as accusing her of being '*a most impious Jezebel*' Whether any of what is said against her, or her husband, was the truth is open to doubt but Waltheof did confess his involvement in the rebellion to an archbishop (no doubt after painful interrogation) and then to William. After imprisonment for a year, he was sentenced to death and his head was removed on 31st May 1076. His much abused body was thrown into a ditch near Winchester.

That might seem the end of the story, but what happened next was even stranger, maybe even incredible.

Many at the time believed Waltheof to have been innocent and it seems that his body was retrieved from the ditch and taken to Crowland Abbey in Lincolnshire where an effigy of what is stated to be him is still occupying a niche. Unfortunately there was a fire in the Chapter House in 1092 and, for some reason, his coffin was opened and lo, a miracle had occurred. The severed head had miraculously reunited itself with the body. The Abbey publicised this widely and it must have come as a great surprise to them that pilgrims and their purses started to find their way to the Abbey, some of whom are attested to have regained their sight! A martyrdom cult developed around Waltheof and a now lost, fictitious, saga was written about him several centuries after his death.

The reason we know about Waltheof and his importance in Hallam is the description in the Domesday Book of 1086. I have tried to make it more understandable so this is an approximate translation and explanation of the contents. The following is what it has to say:-

In Halun (Hallam) there is one manor with 16 hamlets. It has 29 carucates of land (One carucate is usually 120 acres so nearly 3,500 acres of ploughable land) rated as taxable.

There Earl Waltheof had an aula (hall or court)

As many as 20 ploughs possible

Roger de Buesli holds the land of Countess Judith (Waltheof's widow and King William's niece) Roger himself has 2 carucates (240 acres or 2 plough teams) and 33 villeins (householders) hold 12.5 carucates (1,500 acres or 12.5 plough teams)

This would make the wood about 8 miles long and eight miles wide. It is thought that this covered the area of what is now Fulwood.

The whole manor is 10 leagues in length and 8 leagues broad – so 20 miles x 16 miles if a league was indeed 2 miles)

In the time of Edward the Confessor it was valued at 8 Marks of silver, now 40 shillings (a silver Mark was worth 13 shillings and 4 pence so the value had gone down from 106.66 shillings in pre conquest days to 40 shillings in 1086, a reduction to 37.5% of its earlier value in just a little over 20 years.

Those are the bare details, and what they show is that Hallam was an extensive district covering much of the current Westerly and Southerly regions of Sheffield extending north to include what is now Bradfield and south to include what is now Ringinglow. Ecclesall Brierlow was part of a separate district mentioned in Domesday as was Sheafeld and Attercliffe. All were much smaller than Hallam.

According to the excellent Domesday online website (http://www.domesdaybook.co.uk/) the area liable to tax of 29 geld (ploughable) units was very large in comparison to other districts nationally and the 33 households were also larger than in most manors. It is a shame that none of the hamlets mentioned are specifically named in Domesday Book as this would have made identification much easier.

As well as land that could be ploughed there was both pasture land and a wood where animals could graze. In those days cattle would commonly graze in woods.16 hamlets would seem to indicate that there was a significant farming and possibly forestry community in the area. The wooded areas would also have provided hunting sports for the lord. Deer, wild boar and other game would have been encouraged and there may even have been individuals whose responsibility it was to manage these animals. This was certainly the case in later centuries. There is a reference to Fulwood Booth being a place where cattle were kept to supply the local Lord of the Manor in 1181.

I must admit that there is much I find difficult to understand. The two main questions that arise are:-

1   Why, after rebelling in 1069, was Waltheof given additional titles, married to the Conqueror's niece, and allowed to return to that seat of sedition otherwise known as 'the North'? The answer appears to have been that the region was virtually ungovernable and William decided to allow local men who had support in the region to do the job for him. No doubt the marriage to William's niece had the intention of cementing Waltheof to the Norman cause. William had enough on his hands consolidating his position in the more prosperous South, to be over-concerned with the North. What is now called the 'Harrying of the North' by his army in 1069-70 was to prevent that area being able to support further invasion by Norsemen or Danes.

2. The reduction in value of Hallam despite the large number of remaining settlements. It was normal for even prosperous places in the North to see reductions to 40% of pre-conquest values. There are several possible explanations for the reduction in Hallam. The one most often given is that the devastation of the North caused significant destruction of physical assets and widespread depopulation. Apart from the missing aula there is no evidence of any destruction in this region. The tracked progress of William's army (whose responsibility it was to carry out the destruction) shows total devastation of Wales near Rotherham but from there the army moved north towards Wentworth – some way away from Hallam. It may also be relevant that the land is expressed to be held 'of the Countess Judith'. This may mean that some payment or service was due to her by Roger de Buesli which would mean the value of his land was akin to what would now be a tenant's interest which may not have been the case in Edward the Confessor's day. Like may not therefore be being compared with like as we assume.

In addition to the above, it is likely that the whole economy of the North was affected badly by whatever destruction and depopulation there may have been in other parts of the region . No doubt the replacement of many Saxon Earls with Norman overlords, nominated by William, will have meant there were few individuals able to buy land and fewer people to work on the land reducing its economic return. Finally the 'showpiece' Aula was no longer there so I suppose it may not be at all surprising to see a reduction in the value even without any widespread devastation in the area. I would love to know how Burnt Stones near Redmires Road got its name though! The standard explanation is that the name came about as a result of the effects of fires connected with iron smelting out on the crags, but who knows?

It is unlikely that Waltheof ever lived here but he is likely to have hunted and entertained in his Aula in Hallamshire. The Hallamshire name has been used throughout the centuries since, and the most recent hospital and University built in Sheffield were both given the name. Hallam and Hallamshire are well known names in these parts. Waltheof is not. Maybe he should be, as it would seem that he was the first person known to have brought status to this remote area.

Earl Waltheof is commemorated in the old Parish Church of Sheffield . Admittedly it is a 1930's idea of what a Saxon/Norman Earl might like look, but it is the best I have! He stands alongside five other historical figures of Sheffield so is in good company. That shield looks remarkably Norman to me. Somewhat ironic given the number of times he seems to have fought them!

Fig 11
Earl Waltheof
By kind permission of
The Dean and Chapter
of Sheffield Cathedral

CHAPTER 4

<u>DR THOMAS SHORT AND FULWOOD SPA</u>

The whereabouts of the reputed Fulwood Spa have proved something of a challenge to those who have sought this watery miracle and reported their findings in print over the last 200 years

This is what Joseph Hunter has to say about it in his survey of Hallamshire in 1819

'A mineral spring at Fullwood was once of considerable note……. It was much resorted to in 1666, a period of alarm respecting the plague. Dr Short who gives an analysis of its uses says that 'it was of very great note formerly, much frequented , and vast benefit reaped from its' use in all cases wherein light chalybeates takes place. He [Short] had been told that there was once a treatise written upon it but he could not learn when or by whom. It was sometimes called Fullwood Spa or Heaton-Spa from its benefactor Thomas Heaton of Sheffield who laid a bason , built a house over it, and made a way to it from his great philanthropy. The Doctor [Short] recommends that a bath should be constructed near it. Whether this spring ever deserved the reputation it obtained is questionable and what it had obtained it has long lost.'

The Dr Short he refers to was Thomas Short a doctor from Sheffield the author of '*The Natural Experimental and Medicinal History of the Mineral Waters of Derbyshire Lincolnshire and Yorkshire'* published in 1734 but with an address to the President to the Council and Fellows of the Royal Society of London for improving Natural Knowledge dated Sheffield Sept 5th 1733. The book lists many subscribers, amongst them the Duke of Devonshire, the Duke of Rutland, Sir William Wentworth, the Earl of Derby, Sarah Duchess of Marlborough and some lesser known titled individuals like Lord Viscount Primrose and the Right Hon Patee Byng also known as the Lord Viscount Torrington apparently. There are also a lot of famous names from Sheffield history, including Samuel Shore , Thomas Wright and William Jessop of Broomhall

Chalybeate was water rich in iron salts and, from the following description of its uses, sounds as though it was the miracle drug of the 17th and 18th Centuries.

Dudley North the 3rd Baron North was a substantial landowner who discovered such a spring on his own estate and showed it to his physician who was so impressed that, in 1606, he wrote, a treatise extolling the virtues of the Chalybeate spring waters called by him '*Vitriol*' which he claimed cured

'The colic, the melancholy and the vapours, it made the lean, fat and the fat, lean, it killed flatworms in the belly, loosened the clammy humours of the body and dried the over-moist brain'

Now who could have guessed that the vitriol we speak of today could have such effects. In those days it just meant any metallic sulphate rather than the acid tongue of today, no doubt the result of an over-moist brain.

The popularity of Chalybeate lasted well into the 19th Century. Even Queen Victoria would often take such waters. I suspect Royalty did not find its' way to Fulwood Spa that often, but, no doubt, the great and good of the locality came, particularly when they needed protection from the plague at Eyam and the surrounding area or when suffering from an attack of the vapours.

Here is Dr Short's description of the site.

'Fullwood-Spaw or Eaton-Spaw: The first name is from the next village about a mile off: the last from its Benefactor the late Thomas Heaton of Sheffield. It lies about 4 miles South West of Sheffield, rises up on the north side of a most desert heathy mossy mountain , is intensely cold beyond any Chalybeate water yet met with.'

Ivor Gatty, a local historian, was quite definite about the whereabouts of the Spa in 1943. He says that Fulwood village is usually referred to as the area around the junction of Brookhouse Green and Crimicar Lane, now occupied by shops including the Co-op. He says this area is 4.25 miles from the Cathedral just S of a WSW direction, so using Dr Short's measurements, this put the spa somewhere on the Northern slope of the hillside running up from High Storrs to Ringinglow. He selected the origins of the river Porter to investigate, and. in particular, focused on an area known locally as 'The Rough'. He goes on to identify the actual site as follows

'The Porter rises mainly in a small wood known as 'The Clough'. On the East side there is a small piece of land known locally as 'The Rough'. In the NE corner, close to the stream, there stands a piece of square-topped masonry with an opening about 18 inches wide and 16 inches high out of which flows a small stream of water. Behind it the ground rises steeply, covered with coarse grass, heather and a number of small bogs.'

Of course I had to go and see what I could find.

My first attempt found me at one end of the Clough where I negotiated my way down a precipitous slope hanging on to a tree branch and discovered a small spring which made its way down to the river. Whilst attempting to ignore the worried looks of runners and walkers going along the footpath below as I poked with a stick, while hanging on to a branch, all I found was a moderate sized natural stone. Hardly a success!

A few days later, I found Dr Gatty's original article dated June 1943 in Sheffield Archives.

The good Doctor starts by quoting the Sheffield Constable's accounts for the year 1666 which state

'Charges about keeping people from Fullwood Spaw in the tyme that the plague was at Eam.'

Obviously potential plague carriers were not made too welcome by the locals in 1665/6.

Dr Gatty then goes on to comment on the 'housing' of the Spa. He makes the point that as it stands with just the present masonry it would be useless. You could not fill a bucket with it as you could only scoop up a small amount and it would also be a 'complete hindrance' for cattle to drink from.' He believes the housing Dr Short referred to was most likely a simple stone trough with a plain canopy over the top to keep the sides from caving in and animals from sullying the water. The trough or bason as Dr Short described it had vanished but Dr Gatty makes the point that such would have made an excellent hen trough for a local farmer or villager which may explain the absence.

Apparently there was no trace of iron found when the water he took from the stream in 1943 was examined. This he took to be confirmation of that which Hunter had implied. Dr Gatty found deeply stained stones and abundant traces of ochre under the surrounding vegetation that he had pulled away. Whether this amounted to what Dr Short had described as 'The most monstrous amount of ochre' at the site he could not say but he certainly felt it proved that this spring was once iron containing.

Moving down to the nearby river Dr Gatty noted on either side of the Porter, near the spring, there stood the supports for a plank bridge, maybe part of the way that Mr Heaton is reported to have made to the spa.

One of Dr Gatty's correspondents informed him that he knew of the' Rough' stream and had been told that, in the 1840's, the man's Uncle James Broomhead used to go there with a local doctor in a pony and trap to collect spring water for his patients. The correspondent did though claim that he site of the Spa itself was near and below Fulwood Booth, the top and middle Redmires reservoirs being visible from the site. He says the water there was cool in summer and warm in winter and the only place cattle could drink in the exceptionally cold winter of 1895 when all the other springs had frozen over. Dr Gatty also reports that another individual, in a letter to the Sheffield Telegraph, stated that her grandmother used to go to the spring every day from their home at Fulwood Grange Farm for water to help cure her very ill husband . This was in around 1850. She said that it was on the moors beyond Redmires reservoir and it was known locally as St Anne's Well. Both reports sited the well far away from Dr Short's description of the location of the spa, so were dismissed by Dr Gatty as being unlikely candidates. He felt the 'Rough' was more likely. His reasons being fourfold:-

1.   The wellhead was built on unclaimed land. There was no purpose for it otherwise than to enable use of it by visitors.

2.   It was close to Dr Short's description of the whereabouts of the spa.

3.   The Doctor of 1840 used to fetch water from it for his patients.

4.   It was once chalybeate because of the ochre stained stones in and around the watercourse.

The argument sounded plausible so I arranged another Porter trip. The Porter, incidentally, gets its name from the reddish colour of the popular porter beer. Much of the river ran red in the past!

Off the beaten track and through holly, brambles and other natural obstacles I found a spring. Not only that but where it appeared to be emerging from the ground it was certainly red. I certainly could not see any masonry over a foot high nor was there any clear channel down to the river. As the spa site I felt it unlikely,

The spa therefore remained elusive. Good luck if you are tempted to look for it! I would add that J Edward Vickers report of the spa was that it was used by locals and was 'close to' the ecumenical chapel in Fulwood. That description is also used in Sheffield Council's Conservation Area Appraisal dated March 2008 although neither source gives any reason for this assertion.

Fig 12 Restored packhorse bridge

On the way back home from my 2nd trip, I admired the millennium project restoration of the old packhorse bridge over the Porter. I wonder how many, if any, crossed it on the way to the spa, if indeed the spa was ever there?

I am not entirely convinced by Dr Gatty's theory. It rests heavily on the measurement of lines on a map. I do not believe that the original description is likely to come from any of the scanty, and not necessarily to scale, maps available at the time of Dr Short's writings. These are more likely to measure the distance along the convoluted tracks that existed from Sheffield to Fulwood at that time. The 1840 Doctor may well have taken water from 'the Rough' for his patients but that does not prove it was anything other than a spring, or well, of which there are many in the region, that contained iron salts. The masonry is indeed curious but this could have been erected by anyone at any time and there was certainly no evidence of the bason (basin) that was reportedly erected by Thomas Heaton at the spa.

If Gatty was, indeed, incorrect I thought I should widen the search area. I parked in the car park at the top of Clough Plantation and headed through the wood in the opposite direction to the normal Round Walk path. Within about 100 yards I came across what could only be described as a man-made pond filled by a small waterfall coming over an old wall. Following the stream, a little upwards, just beyond the wall, I found it emerged from what looked like a constructed stone opening in a raised, roughly triangular, piece of land that looked as though it was once part of an adjoining farmer's field.

Fig 13

This small pool, part of, and near the source of, a substantial spring that runs into the Porter Brook seems to be man-made. It is below an area of raised walled ground, next to a farmer's field.

The photograph below shows the whole site.

Fig 14

A waterfall flows over the wall that retains a small triangular area of land, at the upper end of the Porter Clough near the Round Walk car park -turn right and follow the path downwards. The spring begins just behind the field wall over which it flows. The pool is at the bottom right of the photograph and drains down a mountainous drop to the Porter below.

In 1740, Dr Short published a further book entitled The Mineral Waters of England Vol 2. Fulwood Spaw is mentioned 3 times in this book. In part 3 the good doctor lists various ailments and the waters that may treat them. It seems that for diseases of the head' the *'plain spirituous steel waters of Fulwood'* are efficacious and if your problems arise from drinking *sharp strong fermented liquor, dramming, whetting, or immoderate Punch drinking*,' then the waters of *Buxton, Althorpe or Fulwood Spaw etc* are the cures for you.

I researched Thomas Heaton a little further and discovered that he and Thomas Short were both initial shareholders in the Company of Proprietors of the Navigation of the River Don which was formed in 1732

So it seems likely that they knew each other and, quite possibly it was Mr Heaton who took Dr Short to the spa and told him of his own building works there.

As to Dr Thomas Short, he was born around 1690 in the south of Scotland. He came to Sheffield to set up his medical practice where he gained a good reputation. Following his death in 1772, volume 100 of the Gentleman's magazine published an appreciation of his life. It recounts that the Marchioness of Rockingham is stated to have indicated at a dinner party that she would trust her life in Dr Short's hands rather than any other of his faculty. A vicar from Worsborough, a Mr Staniland, replied that he did not like the man. When asked *why?* by the Marchioness he is alleged to have replied

'If it had not been for the Doctor I should have been rid of my wife several years ago!'

On the other hand one of his patients an attorney at law is said to have been sent to Leicestershire to take the waters at a particular spring. He did so but unfortunately managed to die on the road home. Not exactly a good advertisement (unless you really don't like lawyers)

The doctor, who apparently exaggerated his Scottish accent, was a somewhat eccentric individual. In his *'Historical Notes of Old Sheffield Druggists'*, John Austen reports that our Doctor slept over a coal house to preserve his lungs and threw porridge dinner parties at which no spoons were provided!
.

As to his family life, this is a sad story. He married Mary Parkins of Mortimley near Sheffield in 1732 and they had four children, two girls and two boys. The boys were, apparently, 'wild' according to a Gentleman's magazine article, but one died young and one died abroad, unmarried, both before their Father. One daughter Mary died in 1753 and the other daughter Elizabeth married a Mr Anderson of Pea Street Sheffield but died without issue in 1788. Mary, his wife, died in December 1762 and Thomas himself in 1722 in Rotherham . They were commemorated with a plaque in the Parish Church in Sheffield

So I leave the good doctor with his words from his *Yorkshire History* about the waters of Fulwood Spa.

'It fits exceedingly light on the stomach, goes quickly off, is a powerful diuretic forcing its way through obstructions, raises the spirits, takes off the gloomy pensive melancholy Clouds and Damps,sets all irregularities of the menses at rights, breaks through removable barriers in the liver, spleen or other viscera. Restores a lost appetite and digestion, clears the stomach kidneys intestines ureters and bladders, helps stuffings and shortness of breath…….. At the side of the Bason (basin) might be made an excellent and first rate cold bath in all the neighbourhood.'

So a bath in the coldest water he has known out on the moors by Fulwood in February is just what you need – if you can ever find the place. A rival to Harrogate or Bath? Maybe not..

CHAPTER 5

FOUR FOXES OF FULWOOD

1. Ulysses Fox

The wonderfully named Ulysses Fox was one of 5 children He was born in 1656 (or, at least that is when he was baptized). Hunter, in his 1819 commentary on Hallamshire, observes that it was somewhat unusual for his yeoman farmer family parents to give their children the names Ulysses, Zacharia, Sophronia and Gertrude. The other was called Sarah, but she was the youngest so they had probably run out of unusual names by then. The family did, though, live in one of the only two houses of note in the region, according to Hunter, so perhaps wanted to impress. Their home was Fullwood Hall. Their son, Ulysses, inherited the Hall in 1612, on the death of his father William Fox, and is responsible for the way the house on Harrison Lane in Fulwood appears today. The 1620 date inscription on the Hall itself commemorates the additions he made in that year to what had been originally a fifteenth century building and the home of the Foxes for several generations before Ulysses and his parents.

The house today is an attractive Grade II listed building, built of local stone, which looks down onto the Mayfield Valley. It retains most of its 17th Century appearance and is best seen, albeit at some distance, from the other side of the valley where the mullioned windows with their diamond shaped small glass panes give the house a look of age and character. It was built in an L shape. Little of the house itself can be seen from Harrison Lane which runs behind the Hall as the house is built somewhat down the hill. I have not been inside so cannot verify it but it is reported to have panelling in some downstairs rooms, an internal Tudor stone doorway and fireplace dating to the pre-Ulysses days. The Hall still bears the name Fullwood Hall on the back gate from Harrison Lane although a single L is normally used these days in the spelling of the region. In referring to the area I have used Fulwood and, in respect of the Hall, Fullwood apart from direct quotations. It really isn't my fault that different generations have insisted on spelling it differently! In his place names of the West Riding of Yorkshire, Part 1, A H Smith lists the following variations of the place namely:

Folwod (Edward II era)

Fulwod and Fulwode (1332)

Fulwudd (1379)

Fullewod in Hallumch'r (1359)

Fullewood (1383)

Fullwod and Fullwood (1366)

Fig 15
Fullwood Hall from Harrison Lane

Ulysses himself seems to have been a wealthy man for, not only did he rebuild the Hall, but he also built a corn mill just down the road and dammed the Mayfield Brook to provide the water power. Many of the associated mill buildings remain though not the water wheel that would have provided the grinding power. The present Animal Sanctuary is what was the old mill house and there is still a row of buildings behind and at right angles to the Animal Sanctuary building. If you look over the wall near the bridge over the Mayfield Brook the shape of the water reservoir can still be made out.

Grinding corn could be a somewhat contentious issue in those days. The Lord of the Manor had a monopoly on mills and grain could only be ground at his mill. This right went back several hundred years. It seems Ulysses and others decided that travelling 4 miles to the nearest flour producing mill was too far for those living in Fulwood and the immediate area and they needed a much more local facility. Unfortunately this ended up in Court and, in 1641, Ulysses was fined £35 8s 9d for trespass against the Lord of the Manor's rights. I suspect he may have felt this was money well spent as the mill seems to have continued in operation and will have provided a good income from charging local farmers for grinding their grain. It is reputed that later in its' life the inventor of Sheffield plate, Thomas Boulsover, sent his plated buttons and snuff boxes to be polished there

A second mill and a separate, adjoining, dam were constructed much later and are now lost, apart from a depression where the water used to be. These are more fully described in David Crossley's excellent book 'Water Power on the Sheffield Rivers' where the two mills are discussed under the River Porter section under the sub-heading 'Fulwood (Mayfield) Corn Mills'. Ulysses was married to Elizabeth from nearby Low Bradfield and they had one son William. Sadly William died in 1648 shortly before his Father. As William had 6 children of his own though, the Fox family continued to live in the Hall until the dissolute days of his grandson, George, early in the next century. His story follows.

2. George Fox (The elder)

George Fox wasted the Estate. That is the information given by Hunter in explanation of George losing the family seat, Fullwood Hall, in 1707. Muriel Hall though is more revealing. In her book' More of Mayfield Valley with Old Fulwood', she reports that George came to inherit the Fulwood Estate at the tender age of 5 on the deaths of his Father, William, in 1646 and Grandfather, Ulysses, in 1649. He could not enjoy possession in his own right until he reached 21, the age of majority. He married Dorothy Balgay in around 1665 when he had reached that age and he moved into Fullwood Hall with his new wife. Somewhat oddly, his wife's father later married George's mother making him both father-in-law and step -father to the young George. Sadly, George's wife died on August 11th 1676 leaving him with 5 young children with an age range of between 2 and 9 years. His eldest son, Henry had died in 1669

George married again in 1679. This may have caused problems for him as his new wife Mary Pole was a Catholic and this would not have gone down well in Fulwood with its large Dissenting community. Nevertheless he fathered 5 more children with his new wife and it seems these children were all brought up as Catholics.

It certainly seems as though George had challenges in his life. Sadly, once he stopped fathering children he appears to have decided not to face up to his responsibilities and he turned to excessive drinking and gambling. Vickers, in his book 'Old and Historic Buildings of Sheffield' states that George and Henry Bright of nearby Whirlow Hall together with Henry Hall of Stumperlowe Hall and several others in the area '*lived a life of gaiety and indulgence such that all of their money wasted away and their estates eventually had to be sold.*' Of Water Carr Hall itself Hunter puts it this way

'*There was a small public house in Fullwood known by the name of Water Carr Hall which was the scene of the wretched man's* (Bright's) *indoor dissipation. At this house he was accustomed to meet Fox of Fullwood Hall and Hall of Whirlow who were running the same road to ruin.*'

Fig 16 Carr Houses today. Water Carr Hall comprised the part on the left between the two old chimneys. It is reputed to have been directly responsible for the loss of the fortunes of the owners of Fulwood Hall, Whirlow Hall and Stumperlowe Hall The separate building behind is the 'Little Mesters' Workshop

Water Carr Hall comprised the first two cottages that now form Carr Houses, the attractive row of 4 cottages on the other side of the road from Carr Bridge. Water Carr Hall had been built in 1675, the two additional cottages and the separate block to the right being built later, well after George's time, as was the stone building slightly behind the row of cottages which was a workshop in the later 1700's of the

'Little Mester' type possibly making files and penknives.

George must have been in substantial debt for when Fulwood Hall was sold to redeem the mortgage. The entire sale proceeds of £800 went to the Mortgagee to pay off the debt

What became of the impoverished George? It is not known. I suspect the following burial record at Sheffield Parish Church – now rather grandly called the Cathedral may be his.

'George Fox- Gent. Died Sheffield buried 29th July 1718 '

If this indeed is the ex-Fulwood Hall George, his grandfather Ulysses was also buried there and memorised on the South side of the porch. George only merits a grave outside

On his seal George had imprinted a bear carrying a battle axe with the motto' And Let God Help.' The bear with an axe seems quite appropriate. Whether he lived by the motto may be open to doubt.

George's son, imaginatively also named George, remained in the area and he turned out to be quite a contrast to his, wastrel Father. Unlike his bear father, the son George does seem to have taken the motto to heart.

3. George Fox (the son)

The younger George was born in 1670 and was the oldest surviving son of the George described above. In 1707 he was a signatory to the Deed transferring Fullwood Hall and his Father's other Fulwood Estate to John Fox to whom he was not related. It seems George had already established himself in the local community by the time of his Father's loss of the Hall and the estate.

In 1699 he had married Ann Broomhead the daughter of John Broomhead, a substantial landowner in the area and a family that still has descendants here.

In contrast to his Catholic step mother and her children, his half brothers and sisters, the younger George seems to have been a respected member of the local Dissenting community. He was named as an executor in the will of the local benefactor William Ronksley in 1723 and was appointed one of the first Trustees of the Dissenters' chapel built in Fulwood in 1728. It is probable that he acted as Guardian to William Ronksley's two young nephews who were their Uncle's main beneficiaries under his will. George had two children, George, son of George, (also son of George), was baptised in 1702 at the Upper Chapel in Sheffield ,and John, who it is reported to have been living at Towton in the parish of Attenborough in the county of Nottingham in 1717 . He was stated to be a minor and working as 'a frame-work knitter'.

The George (the subject of this section) died in or around 1739. His widow Ann survived him by 21 years.

4. John Fox

John Fox bought Fullwood Hall from the George Foxes in 1707. He paid the sum of £800 for the Hall and substantial other holdings in the area, John and George (Junior) were from completely different families. George was of Yeoman farmer stock from Fullwood Hall whereas John's family went back to a William Fox who was a charcoal burner at Beauchief (post reformation) in 1560. It does not seem as though John's family had any substantial connection with Fulwood. John had a house on Dixon Lane in Sheffield which displayed as his Coat of Arms a chevron with three foxes' heads.

John and the younger George did have one thing in common. They shared a common outlook on religious matters and, as Dissenters, both contributed significantly to the development of Fulwood .

John Fox never married, and, unusually, the best way to understand him is through his death. His Will, dated 9th November 1720 sheds light on much that was happening in the region at that time and the concerns of a nonconformist man of property with no wife or children, so I am reciting it in some detail – for which I make all suitable apologies.

John's begins his Will with the formulaic words "In the name of God Amen" This was a standard introduction to wills for those times. He then describes himself as "John Fox of Fullwood Hall in the parish of Sheffield in the county of York Gent being of sound and disposing mind and memory" Throughout his will he spells Fulwood with two L's as it still is on the Harrison Lane gate sign outside the house today.

The Executors he appointed were William Wadsworth, William's son John Wadsworth, a preacher in the Upper Meeting House in Sheffield, now the Unitarian Upper Chapel), Samuel Shore and Benjamin Greaves. The appointment of John Wadsworth as Minister in Sheffield in 1715 had caused a split in the Non-Conformist congregation with 200 of the more extreme members departing to found the Nether Chapel in Sheffield. John Fox seems to have remained with the majority and backed the Trustees choice of John Wadsworth as Minister.

He makes various gifts of money to his closest relatives and their children, then comes the following section of his will:-

"Unto my cousin John Webster £10 to buy him mourning and I give to the poor people in Mr Holley his hospital 40 shillings (£2) to be equally divided amongst them upon Christmas day next after my death and I give to the Trustees for the use of the hospital the sum of £40 if I shall not have given them that sum in my lifetime And I devise to the Trustees of the Charity school at Sheffield for the use of the said Charity school the sum of £40 if I shall not have given them that sum in my lifetime"

He makes several other gifts of £10 'for mourning' which indicates his family may not have been wealthy (or that he wanted at least a few of them at his funeral). One cousin, also called John Fox, was described as residing at Beauchief Hall – it seems he was farming there. The charitable gifts were considerable amounts for those times and I like the idea of dispensing money to the poor on Christmas day. I always thought it was the Victorians who 'invented' gifts at Christmas!

Religion played an important part in John Fox's life. He was a Dissenter which meant that, although a Protestant, he did not accept the Church of England as having sole authority to interpret and express the true word of God. Prior to the Act of Toleration in 1688 the provisions of the 1662 Act of Uniformity (the fourth in a series of such Acts) and the 1665 'The 5 Mile Act' were still largely in force meaning that no non-conformist minister could preach or come within 5 miles of a town. Fulwood lay just outside this distance from Sheffield (if you allow for the difficulties of there being no direct road). and so seems to have become a place frequented by Dissenters where they could hear the word of God preached by ministers who had been expelled from the Establishment Church following the passing of those Acts. By the time John Fox had bought Fullwood Hall in 1707 the 1689 Act of Toleration, following William 111's accession, had mitigated the worst of the restrictions on ministers and most non-conformists could preach as long as they were prepared to swear an oath of allegiance to the Crown and that their meeting places were licensed. Religious meetings in private houses were forbidden unless the premises were licensed in much the same way public houses are licensed today. By 1714 John Fox had applied successfully for a licence to allow an upper room in Fulwood Hall to be used as a place of worship for Dissenters who had previously to brave the wilds of the nearby moors to worship in outdoor or out of the way places like Lords Seat (near where Stanedge Pole is now) or travel into Sheffield itself once the Upper Meeting room there had been licenced. No doubt the many Dissenters in the region praised the Lord that they could, at last, worship indoors without a lengthy journey. It is not therefore surprising that, returning to his will, he makes the following bequest:-

" I devise the sum of £100 and will that my Executors within 12 months after my decease lay out that sum in purchasing lands of inheritance to be settled on the Trustees of the Upper or Great Meeting House in Sheffield where Mr Wadsworth is now minister and their heirs and successors to the use and in trust to apply the rents and profits thereof to the said Mr Wadsworth and his successors in the said meetinghouse forever for the preaching lecture or sermon in the said meeting house every other Sunday or Lords day in the evening throughout the year for ever"

In other words here is some money to help buy property and you can use the rents to help pay the preacher in Sheffield! It is slightly odd that he makes no mention of continuation of worship at Fulwood Hall and this may help explain why, a few years later, one of John's friends and early co-worshipers at Fulwood Hall (and presumably earlier out on the moors), William Ronksley, left money for a more substantial place of worship to be built in Fulwood itself and what is now the Unitarian chapel on Whiteley Road was built in 1728.

John did not neglect the inhabitants of Fulwood. He gives money to the local school.

"I will and devise that my Executors within the span of 12 months or so soon after my death as conveniently may be to lay out the sum of £100 in the purchase of lands tenements and hereditaments of Inheritance to be settled and secured to the use of and for and towards the perpetual maintenance of a schoolmaster to teach and instruct children to read and write in the now erected school in or near Fulwood aforesaid "

The school he referred to was the school from which School Green Lane is named. This building is now a private house but bears a plaque (illustrated below) upon which is inscribed:-

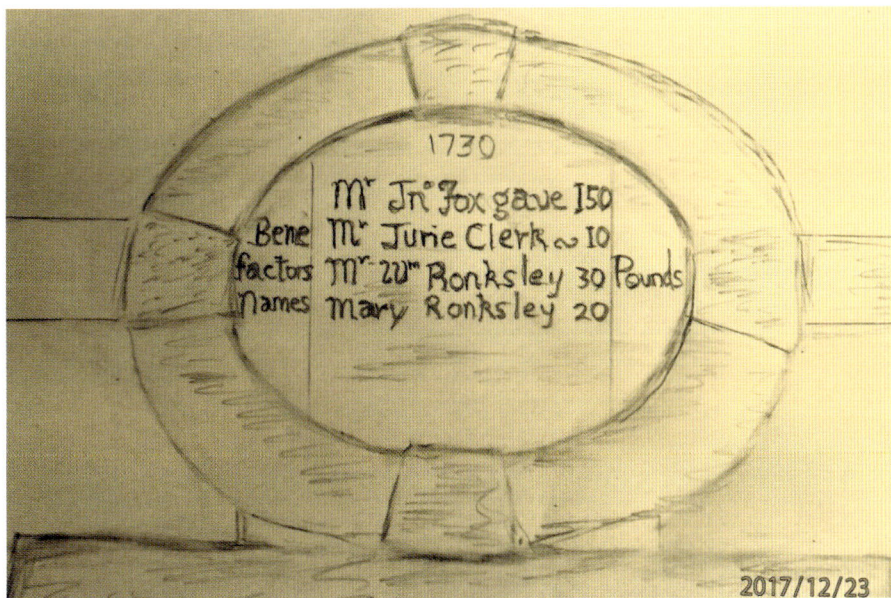

Fig 17

Drawing of plaque on Former school on School Green Lane

1730

Benefactors

Mr. John Fox gave 150 pounds

Mr Jurie Clerk 10 pounds

Mr William Ronksley 30 pounds

Mary Ronksley 20 pounds

It therefore looks likely that John gave an extra £50 to the school during his lifetime which was probably used to build it in 1720. The Report of the Commissioners for inquiry concerning charities refers to the school as follows:-

Fulwood school founded by John Fox in 1720 and augmented by the will of William Ronksley dated 9th October 1723 – Endowed with 4 Acres of land. 18 Free scholars taught reading and writing.

All the books I have read give the date of the school construction as 1730 because of the plaque's inscription date, yet it seems it must have been much earlier because John describes the school as 'now erected' in November 1720 being the date of his will. The chapel on Whiteley Lane has a similarly styled inscription and there is argument as to whether that date is also incorrect!

Robert Jurie Clerk was a clerk in holy orders, the incumbent at Ecclesall Church, which explains the 'Clerk' reference. The plaque itself was erected when the single storey school was deemed both too small and also in poor repair so closed in 1792 when a larger school was built on adjoining land and the original building extended. The old school then became a home for the master. It appears that a Benjamin Ashton of Hathersage also gave £5 to the school but his name obviously failed to make it onto the plaque.

The School Green Lane school was built on waste land of the Manor for which the trustees paid one shilling a year. There is a tale worthy of Charles Dickens relating to this school complete with poor children, a wicked landlord and a schoolmaster of questionable morals, but all this will be told in full later In the chapter relating to the Petition!

Fig 18

The school masters house and former school on Old School Lane in Fulwood.

CHAPTER 6

<u>WILLIAM RONKSLEY AND THE CHAPEL</u>

William Ronksley and John Fox are probably the two greatest benefactors that Fulwood has known. William Ronksley was born in Fulwood in around 1650 and seems to have retained a great affection for the place even though his adult life took him to many different places as a tutor and teacher including Hathersage in Derbyshire and Gunthwaite near Penistone where he was living at the time of his death.

Before describing the benefits he gave to the local community (which is all that is usually said of him) I would like to give some idea of the man himself. Growing up in Fulwood in the second half of the seventeenth century it will come as no surprise that he was a religious Dissenter. What may surprise many though is how progressive his views on education were, not only for the early eighteenth century, but even for today, many of his ideas are worthy of consideration.

In 1712 he wrote *The Child's Week's Work* which illustrates his belief that children learning to read, do so more quickly through poetry than through prose, once they had learned to sound their letters. His work states that two hours in the morning and two in the afternoon will be quite sufficient leaving them plenty of time to play between lessons. The Oxford Handbook to British Poetry 1660 – 1800 states that, for Ronksley, reading begins at an age when a child's "*gay and airy tempers*" made the '*enjoyment of serious topics wittily or elegantly expressed* 'beyond them and simple rhymes would guide them more effectively "*through wisdom's door*" with age-appropriate rhymes. The following is an example

> *Gloves for the Hands,*
> *Our Necks have Bands*
> *The head is deckt with Hair:*
> *Some Masks the Face,*
> *And so no place, or part,*
> *Is left quite bare.*

His claim that a child could read almost any book written in English by the end of a five week course employing these methods may seem a tad over-inflated but I suppose he had to sell his book somehow. The point he makes about traditional schooling taking children through the experience of learning to read as their "*old rough melancholy trod*" may ring a bell with some of us though. He also makes an analogy to his system being akin to a walker that a child uses to learn to walk until it is no longer necessary. This illustrates that here was a man who understood children. He was apparently quite strict in his lessons but he seems to have wanted to bring out the best in those in his care.

Like John Fox, his contemporary, and I believe his friend, his generosity is most exemplified by his will which was made in September 1723 shortly before his death on January 4th 1724. In this document he shows his gratitude to Fulwood, '*the place of my nativity*' which he mentions specifically by name. It does not seem that he was aware of the school that John Fox had founded in 1720 in School Green Lane (probably because he had been living in Gunthwaite for many years at the time and John had died shortly after the school was built) for he makes a gift of £30:

'To be paid 3 years after my decease to and for the use of a school in Fulwood ... for ever for which four children of the poorer sort shall be taught to read English only to be chosen out of Fulwood aforesaid by [my nephews] ...which school I would have to be on or near to Birks Green that is near to John Broomhead's house, if the neighbours think good.'

Birks Green is both an area and, according to Muriel Hall, the old name for the house there now called Bennet Grange which acquired its new name in 1790. Both the house and the area are some way away from School Green Lane and it seems as though his Trustees decided to give the £30 to the existing school as commemorated by the plaque outside the house on School Green Lane that once housed the school. It is interesting that he considered what John Broomhead's neighbours might think of the idea of a school on their doorsteps. Again this points to a man who considered others as well as helping those who were not able to help themselves because they could not afford education for their children.

The Trusts on which the chapel are held are those set out in William Ronksley's will which left £400 to be invested for four or five years the interest from which was to enable land to be purchased and the building constructed with seats and a pulpit, for dissenting worship. At that time, Fulwood was, in his words, 'remote from church or chapel'.

Fig 19 a The Unitarian chapel today below— b The stocks

The outside of the chapel is little changed from the time it was built. Fulwood stocks were moved and re-erected outside the chapel and are just visible in the photograph. Birk's Green was their original home. Apparently the stone posts were being used as local gateposts before reassembly with new wooden slats. At one time the stocks stood on Brookhouse Green, in the area of the shops at the bottom of what is now Crimicar Lane. This was one of several greens lost as a result of the local Enclosure Acts. It may be that either or both of the original sites reported are incorrect, but who knows?

It is not known if, at the time of Ronksley's death, Dissenters were still worshiping in the upstairs room in Fullwood Hall. Although John Fox's Trustees were certainly Dissenters it is not known whether John's niece and beneficiary of Fulwood Hall, Dorothy was happy with this arrangement. Certainly the Will makes no provision for the meetings to continue, so there must have been uncertainty at the time and a new purpose built chapel must have come as a great relief. The capital of £400 was intended to be invested and to pay the minister out of the income. Unfortunately the sum was wholly lost in a bank crash in the next century, but it was replaced by donations to enable the chapel to survive. For those that do not know, even today it welcomes those of any or no faith - a refreshing approach in these times when religious dogma often seems to spread more hatred than love.

Fig 20 The Minister's House adjoining the chapel

A Minister's house was constructed in 1754. which physically adjoins the chapel. A schoolroom was added on the other side of the chapel, at the same time. Apparently a graveyard existed outside the chapel and bones were found when Whiteley Lane was being widened in 1929, A combination of the road widening, the making of a garden in front of the chapel, a sizeable quarry and landscaping after the quarry ceased to be operational have since removed all trace.

The inside of the chapel has been much altered over the years. The windows in the North wall are deliberately splayed to let in maximum light. It seems the original pulpit was sited between these windows and faced high backed wooden box pews where the congregation were able to sit in reasonable comfort.

Services are still held in the chapel every Sunday at 11.00 and more information about the chapel itself is contained in a short 'Welcome' booklet available in the chapel.

William Ronksley has left us a fine legacy. The trusts on which the chapel operates are still those set out in his Will. Fulwood itself is an area that was more or less ignored by the established church until as late as the early 1830's. Although it has not always been operational since 1728, Fulwood Old Chapel has certainly played an important part in maintaining and developing the spiritual life of this region.

CHAPTER 7

JAMES WILKINSON AND THE HALLAM ENCLOSURE RIOT

In the Sheffield stocks, a seven year old girl sat weeping.

What had been her crime?

She had been taught a little rhyme by some older than herself and, at their request, had gone up to a respectable looking clerical man and repeated it to him. This was the harmless sounding rhyme:

'They burnt his books
And scared his rooks
And set his stacks on fire'

The man had asked her to repeat it. When she did, he took her by the hand and led her straight to the stocks where he had her incarcerated.

He was none other than the Vicar of Sheffield and also the chief Magistrate, James Wilkinson as well as self-appointed judge and jury for the poor girl.

The story (originally told by Leader) is related in David Bentley's book *'The Sheffield Hanged'* as a postscript to his section about the hanging of John Benet, an eighteen year old apprentice on Saturday 6th September 1791 for his alleged part in the riots in Sheffield earlier that year. One of those against whom the rioters had vented their anger had been none other than the same James Wilkinson. He did not take kindly to the girl's reminder to him of the night of Monday July 27th 1791

The chain of events that led to what occurred that night can be traced back to Hallam.

In the previous June, 6,000 acres of land over which ordinary, non land-owning people had enjoyed rights of sport and recreation, rights of way and for pasture for their geese and other animals and even the custom of picking blackberries and bilberries for as long as any could remember, were to be apportioned between the landowners of the region freed from those rights. As mentioned elsewhere in this book, the main beneficiary of the 1791 Act for the enclosure of Upper and Nether Hallam was the Duke of Norfolk, but a certain James Wilkinson also stood to gain 12 acres of land as one of the recipients of tithes in the area jointly with Philip Gell who also was to receive land. They were to be compensated by the outright allocation of the land to them free of all local rights.

The following is an extract from the notice about the initial survey contained in the Sheffield Register of 24th June 1791

"…… And the said commissioners do hereby give further notice that they do intend to meet at the sign of the Sun, Bentsgreen in Ecclesall on Wednesday the thirteenth day of July next, at ten o'clock in the forenoon, for the purpose of beginning the perambulation of the OUT-BOUNDARIES of the said commons and waste grounds, within the said several townships, where all persons interested or concerned therein are defined."

The Commissioners, due to meet at the Rising Sun, intending to ride and survey the boundaries were the same James Wilkinson, Vincent Eyre (the Duke of Norfolk's Land Agent) and Joseph Ward, the Master Cutler. It is reported that when they arrived on July 13th they were met with many angry, aproned cutlery workers who expressed their displeasure amid threats of violence to the Commissioners if they were still minded to carry out their stated intention. Hardly surprisingly the local worthies decided to ride quickly back to Sheffield where, fearing an uprising after several other incidents, they summoned military aid from the Government and a troop of Dragoons were dispatched arriving in Sheffield on 27th July.

The population of Upper and Nether Hallam were certainly unhappy as they stood to lose many of their historic rights from enclosure. The townspeople also stood to lose. A popular racecourse existed at Crookesmoor but had already been lost in the Ecclesall Bierlow enclosures according to David Price, in his book' *Sheffield Troublemakers: Rebels and Radicals in Sheffield History.'* Apprentices,who often worked in grim conditions in the town, were used to travelling out to the open countryside to the West of Sheffield where they could enjoy fresh air and exercise. Shooting was also popular. When it seemed inevitable that the plans were going to come into effect and individuals' rights and pastimes were going to be seriously affected, there was much discontent. According to David Bentley, the Times reported that the workers were so enraged by the planned enclosures in Hallam that many adopted the slogan *'Liberty or Death'* for their protest. It must be remembered that the French Revolution was a very recent event and it was thought possible that a similar popular uprising could also occur in Britain.

It was against this background that a large number of people headed for Sheffield in July 1791. They were possibly attracted by the reports of the arrival of the Dragoons. By 9 o'clock that evening there were several hundred people outside the Tontine Inn in Dixon Lane. One of those present was recognized by the Bailiff of the Debtors' Jail and promptly arrested. The crowd took exception to this and freed the man. The Bailiff, rather unwisely, pursued the man and rearrested him. This act sparked the beginning of mob violence. After freeing the man again, the mob pursued the Bailiff to the Debtors' Jail where they pelted it with paving stones and broke down the gates demanding the keys from the Bailiff, who had retreated to his house inside the jail. Once the keys were supplied all the prisoners were released by the mob. At this point the Dragoons arrived and the crowd dispersed

Encouraged by their success, it seems the rioters reassembled and decided on their next target, Broom Hall, the home of James Wilkinson. He had a reputation as a harsh Magistrate and had been instrumental in the presentation of the hated Enclosure Act to Parliament. The Sheffield Register's account of what happened next is as follows:-

'The unthinking multitude, thus successful in their first outrage, pursued their violence. Broom Hall was now the cry – the house of Rev. Mr. Wilkinson our vicar. All his windows were broken, part of his furniture and library damaged and burnt, and eight hay ricks set fire to, four of which were entirely consumed. Before the populace had been too long at Broom Hall, they were followed by the Light Horse who presently dispersed them.'

Some of the rioters moved on to the Duke of Norfolk's land agent, Vincent Eyre's house but -little damage was caused there, Broom Hall being the main sufferer of the effects of the riot. The fires in the downstairs rooms started by the rioters were put out by a neighbour but the incident had a serious effect on James Wilkinson. The incident with the little girl described at the beginning of this tale shows how seriously the riot had affected him.

Several young men were arrested in connection with the rioting, none older than 18. John Benet was convicted and hanged in York for his part in the rioting and arson at Broom Hall. According to David Bentley, the evidence against him was slender, the main witness for the prosecution being another young man who had been charged as a result of John Benet informing the authorities about him. John had several things that worked against him. First, the authorities wished to mete out severe punishment as a disincentive to others in Sheffield who may have considered further riots. Secondly, he was the first to be tried. The others facing trial with him were acquitted. Thirdly the French Revolution had stirred up considerable fear in those who were in a position of power and who dreaded a similar uprising in Britain. John still had 3 years to serve as an apprentice. His Master said he would take him back if John was acquitted as he was a reliable worker but this did not spare him and on 6th September 1791 his life was ended by the noose tightening around his young neck.

Despite popular resentment the enclosures went ahead, even if a little later than planned. If you look at a large scale OS map of this region you will notice a large number of rectangular walled fields. Most of these were created as a result of the allocation of the 6,000 acres under the private Act of Parliament, the1791 Enclosure Act, relating to land in Upper and Nether Hallam.

The poor did get something in return for their loss of several Village Greens, rights of pasture, footpaths, and other areas for sport and recreation. They were given just two acres. Presumably only the land no –one else wanted! A draft of the plan prepared by the Fairbanks, a well-known and respected firm of Surveyors in Sheffield is still available in the Sheffield Archives.

James Wilkinson's Ministry of the church in Sheffield continued from 1754 until his death in 1805. He never married and enjoyed the typical clerical pastimes of hunting and boxing. A sizeable memorial to him was placed in the Cathedral after his death, even though he allowed the church to fall into serious disrepair, the nave only being replaced shortly after his death in 1805. If you take the trouble to visit the Cathedral and find the memorial, you will see, above his head, what I take to be a hangman's noose!

His *'inflexible integrity'* is commemorated in his memorial, whereas the' Alehouse Poet' Joseph Mather described him as *'that black diabolical fiend'*

It sounds as though contemporary views of him depended on whether you were one of the establishment who felt he upheld the social status quo with *'a benevolent disposition'* or one of those likely to be judged by him, who complained of his severity.

In his later years, it seems he had a minor paralysis that earned him the unfortunate nickname amongst those of the latter group, of *'Old Niddlety Nod'*. I do not know whether the events of 1791 contributed in any way to this affliction.

Fig 21 Bust of James Wilkinson Vicar and Chief Magistrate of SheffieldBy kind permission of The Dean and Chapter of Sheffield Cathedral

I bet I know which view the little girl in the stocks had of him though!

Whatever the correct view of him, his presence as Vicar for over 50 years and Chief Magistrate certainly makes him one of the important figures of his era .

He was certainly instrumental in changing Hallam and the way the landscape and fields look today. Without him I might even still have my herbage rights!

CHAPTER 8

<u>THOMAS PEARSON AND THE PETITION</u>

It is the 1st day of September in the year 1828. It looks bleak, indeed, for us poor, beleaguered Trustees of the school in Fulwood as we ponder the future after the children return from the harvest expecting to go back to their school.

Back in 1720 John Fox from Fulwood Hall had paid £50 to erect a school for the poor children of Fulwood. He was nearing the end of his life and he decided to give a further £100, in his will, to be invested with the income earned being used to pay a schoolmaster's salary. His friend William Ronksley had left £30 in his will and William's sister Mary gave a further £20. A clerk in holy orders Robert Jurie had given £10 and Mr B Ashton had provided £5. The investments were bringing in 13 Guineas a year and this was sufficient to pay for a Master to teach the children of the area.

The school has gone from strength to strength, so much so that in 1792 the Trustees decided the single storied school was too small and in need of repair so local volunteers had helped to build a larger schoolroom and convert the old one into a comfortable residence for the Master. The children had a substantial playground as the site covered around 1/3rd of an acre.

The buildings had been put up on what was waste land of the Manor. The owner was his Grace the Duke of Norfolk to whom the Trustees had paid the princely sum of one shilling every year in acknowledgement of his right of ownership.

The old Duke had died in 1815. He was unpopular locally. He had taken the nearby Village Green at Brookhouse Green under the 1791 Private Act of Parliament allowing enclosure of waste grounds and common fields. He had something of a reputation in this respect. He had acquired considerable amounts of land locally to add to his already substantial holdings. We had not foreseen how this could possibly affect the school or ourselves in our position as Trustees

What the old Duke had done before he died was to instruct his local Surveyor, Fairbanks, to prepare plans for selling off some of his land. School Green Farm was one such holding that he wanted to sell. He had not thought to notify the School Trustees of his intentions and we were not aware that the land the school had been built upon was included in the plans as part of the land to be sold and it had been sold to a Mr Thomas Pearson, a wealthy wine and spirit merchant and not a local man. The sale price was £1,400 and for this Mr Pearson had obtained some thirty three and a half acres of land most of which was farmed by the Barber family and for which they paid rent. Unfortunately for the Trustees the sale included the waste land upon which the school buildings and playground stood. If we had known of the intended sale we would have offered to buy the land we occupy.

Now Mr Pearson had, at first, seemed a decent sort. He did not live here as he had bought the land as n investment. He had even lent us £30 to finish repairs to the Masters house once we had acquainted him of the position and at the Duke of Norfolk's office he said he was happy to grant us a very long lease of 999 years at the existing rent of one shilling a year. We have repaid him the £30 and even got as far as going to his attorneys office to get the lease sorted out. At this time, although the sale had been agreed to Mr Pearson, the Conveyance had not been signed by the Duke. A Mr Johnson was then working in the Duke's office and prevented us from entering the attorney's office by saying he could get the matter resolved much more cheaply so we trusted him and left the matter in his hands.

The reason we are now so despondent is that we have been too trusting and are now in the following position :-

1.   The wall dividing the School from School Green Farm has been pulled down and the tenant farmer Mr Barber is now using the land as part of his fields

2.   We have had to dismiss the Master for neglect of duty

3.   Mr Pearson has served us with notice to quit which expires on the 29th of this month

4.   Mr Pearson has applied for a liquor licence for the premises and fixed the appropriate notice to the door of the Parish Church in Sheffield. The Brewster sessions at which the application is due to be heard is fixed for next Wednesday.

5.   The Master is refusing to hand over the keys of the house to us. He says he will only hand them to Mr Pearson. We believe the Master has been promised the tenancy of the Public House if the application is granted.

Mr Thomas Pearson however now sits handsomely in his new home, Leader House in Surrey Street Sheffield which he bought back in 1817. He surely does not need the money, so why is he seeking to deprive the poor children of Fulwood and Hallam of their education and replacing an institution dedicated to improve their morals with one that will corrupt them?

We did attempt to contact Mr Johnson the Duke's then employee but he had left the Duke's employment and when confronted replied that he had made no memorandum of the matter and therefore could not assist. We went to Mr Pearson who was still amiable at that time and said that he could not give us a lease until such time as he had the Conveyance to him signed by the Duke and which he was still awaiting. So we let the matter lie and now find ourselves in our present predicament.

We, the Trustees, are not blameless in this. As well as being too trusting we are responsible for the decision not to pay the one shilling rent to Mr Pearson until he had made good his promise to grant us the 999 year lease. As a result 16 years rent went unpaid, This sum has now been paid in full but it has not relieved us from our present distress.

We are now in God's hands. After much discussion we have decided that the only course open to us is to petition the 12th Duke. He is well known as a staunch Catholic so we have had to play down the Dissenters' role in setting up the school and appointment of Masters etc. The Petition, signed by 43 of us including all five of us School Trustees, Ias well as the local Chapel Warden, the Vicar of Sheffield, the two witnesses who were there in the Duke's office when Mr Pearson promised us the Lease and some of the fathers and grandfathers of the children who may lose their education here, is now ready to be delivered and we consign it with all speed to the Duke's office.

We worry about the last few paragraphs now reproduced here. The Duke may think us as impertinent, but what do we have we to lose by asking the Duke for a new school if we lose the present one? Matters are desperate indeed.

………..But should your Grace think proper to intervene in the manner pointed out above or interfering should prove unsuccessful yet we are confident from your Grace's known kindness and benevolence that now the facts are submitted to your Grace's attention, you will not suffer those premises which were built for education of poor children by the pecuniary subscription of some and by the labour of others, to be abolished without letting Fulwood have another School, School Master's House and Play Ground for the children.

Neither will your Grace allow the endowment to become useless and the children in ignorance but will show your Noble Bounty by causing the erection of other Buildings equally convenient wherein children can receive a sound ,successful education

We crave your Grace's helping hand and we will ever pray for your welfare.
Fulwood 1st Sept 1828

Signatories

John Pitchford	*Witness to what is said regarding the Lease of 999 years*
Thos Creswick	*Witness to what is said regarding the Lease of 999 years*
Edward Wardlow	*Trustee*
John Broomhead	*Trustee*
Stephen Fox	*Trustee and Chapel Warden*
David Woodhouse	*Trustee*
William Tompson	*Trustee*
M G Rhodes	*Dissenting Minister of Fulwood*
Joseph Hallam	
Thomas Sutton	*Vicar of Sheffield*

There follow 33 more signatures both within and upon the backsheet of the Petition written on parchment— as shown in the photograph below of the document in the collection of Sheffield Archives

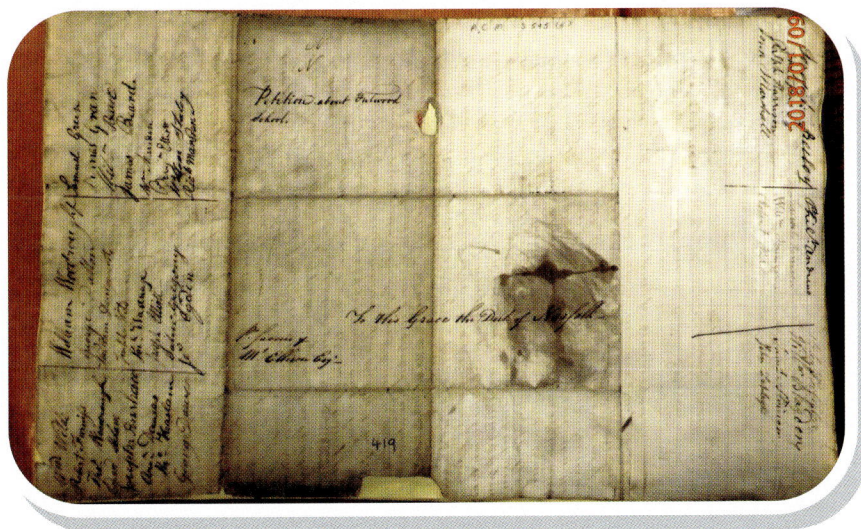

Fig 22

The backsheet of the original Petition to the Duke of Norfolk signed by the school Trustees and local inhabitants of Fulwood

With thanks to Sheffield City Archives for their permission to print the above photograph which bears their reference ACM/21/1/5 (alt ref ACM/S/545/5) and to ACM (Arundel Castle Manuscripts) reproduced with permission from His Grace the Duke of Norfolk, DL.

The outcome of this tale is supplied overleaf.

The Outcome

The tale is a synopsis of what is said in the petition (which is available in the original parchment form in the Sheffield Archives.) It shows a time when the old aristocratic families, after acquiring considerable extra land under the Enclosure Acts, were beginning to sell some of their estates. Property was being bought by the new merchant class and the tale illustrates some of the problems that must have arisen throughout the country at that time, given the informal arrangements that had long existed between local institutions and their land-owning Lords.

There is no exaggeration in the tale. All the material facts are taken directly from my transcription of the petition. The Dukes of Norfolk, Thomas Pearson (although he is referred to throughout just as Mr Pearson), the somewhat shady clerk Mr Johnson, the teacher and would-be publican, and even the part about the licence application being affixed to the church door in Sheffield are all narrated in the petition to the Duke as well as the history of the school, including full details of all the donors, and confirmation that the plaque was put up in 1792 when the old schoolhouse was converted into the Master's residence.

The petition does not name the Farm but local historian Colin Cooper has done considerable research into School Green Farm which he categorically states was bought by Thomas Pearson, wine and spirit merchant, from the Duke of Norfolk in 1813 as 'an investment'. The Barbers remaining as tenant farmers.

The purchase of Leader House in Surrey Street by the same Thomas Pearson in 1817 was a chance discovery but I included mention of it in the tale as this was a very prestigious building, somewhat ironically, originally built on the Duke of Norfolk's orders possibly to provide a residence for his clerk Mr Eyre in 1770.

The Pearsons were the first family to occupy the house after it was sold by the Leader family of silversmiths and this, perhaps, gives some idea of the wealth of Mr Pearson. I would love to know what changed his mind about turning the school into a licensed establishment. Was it conscience? Did money change hands to encourage him to forget the matter?

I do not know what happened but can say that the school was not turned into a public house to corrupt the morals of those in Fulwood, as dreaded by the Trustees in their petition. The locals were quite capable of doing that themselves without outside aid. Maybe the Duke of Norfolk exerted pressure on Mr Pearson or maybe his licence application was unsuccessful and he lost interest in the project. Whatever happened matters seem to have been resolved and the school survived until 1875 when, upon the death of its long serving master, it was decided that a suitably qualified replacement could not be found given the insufficiency of the income that would have had to pay his or her salary. The old Master's House is now a private house as appears to be the single storied, later schoolroom erected nearby on the other side of, what was once, the childrens'playground.

Below is the first Ordnance Survey map of the area, surveyed in 1850/1 and published in 1854

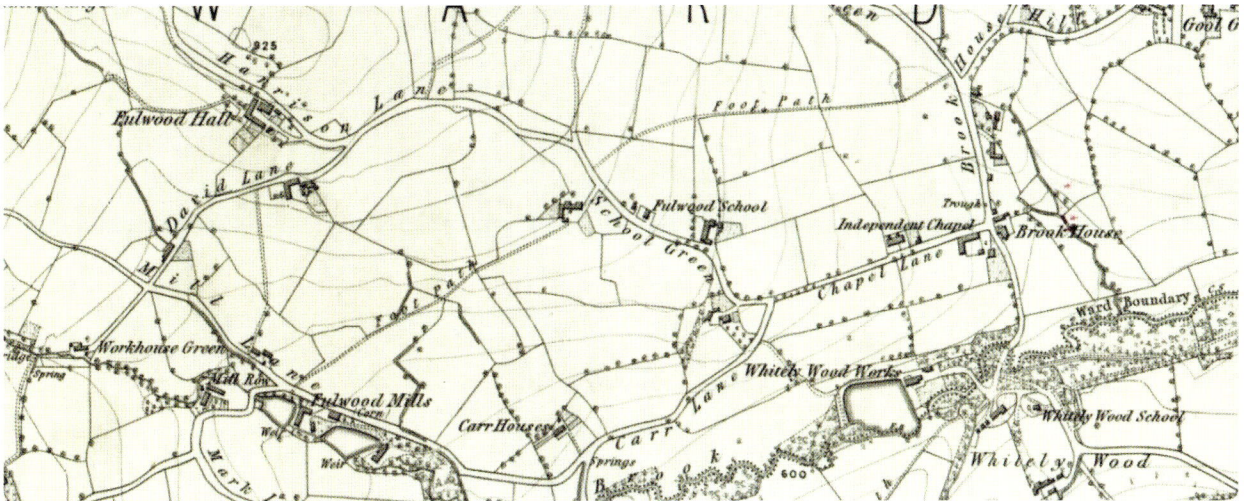

Fig 23 Extract from the 1854 OS map Sheet 294
Reproduced under licence

The original school and the Masters' House are shown as the buildings just above the two O's in *School Green Lane*. School Green Farm, the home of the Barbers is the large building immediately beneath the words *Fulwood School*. The map also shows Fullwood Hall, the home of the Foxes, Fulwood Mills, the first of which was the Corn Mill built by Ulysses Fox, Carr Houses (formerly Water Carr Hall) which contributed to the downfall of the Foxes, the Halls and the Brights, and the Independent Chapel. It also shows how few buildings there were in the area as recently as the early 1850's.

Not far from Fulwood Mills, is an area called *Workhouse Green.* There was never a grim Victorian workhouse here though. Instead there were four workhouse cottages. They are still there, down an unmade lane, near the Mayfield Beck. Not much is known about them, but I have discovered that they were sold by the Overseers of the Poor of Upper Hallam in 1862 to a local farmer, John Broomhead, for £160. The Conveyance recites that the land was originally bought in 1813 and conveyed to the then

Chapel warden and two of the Overseers of the Poor named Daniel Holy and Farewell Harrison, the landlord of the Blacksmiths Arms at Goole Green (part of Ranmoor) and their successors, '*To be used as a workhouse for the accommodation and reception of the poor of the Township of Upper Hallam'* That use lasted under 50 years. The Workhouse erected in Nether Edge, by 1844, on the site of the later hospital was much more the typically grim

Fig 24 Workhouse Cottages today

Victorian Institution and the future destination of the poor people of Upper Hallam!

CHAPTER 9

<u>THE TOOTING TAXMAN AND UPPER HALLAM</u>

The region known as Upper Hallam (shown edged purple on the map at the beginning of this book) comprised a considerable area covering the south-western parts of Sheffield now known as Fulwood, Nether Green, Ranmoor, Carsick Hill, Stephen Hill, Sandygate, Stumperlowe, Ringinglow, Hangingwater and a place described as Crosshack. (Crosspool?) Stanedge Pole was the Western edge with Ringinglow being the most southerly point and the Porter Brook forming the rest of the south and the banks of the Rivelin broadly defining the northern boundary. It was one of the six Townships that comprised Sheffield. It was by far the largest comprising a great area of unenclosed moorland and also one of the least populous.

Although not a subject that leaps off the page with fascination for most people, taxation records can provide an excellent picture of a place and its inhabitants at a particular moment in time. Domesday Book gives us such a window upon Hallamshire in 1087. Almost 600 years later, in 1672 It does again for Upper Hallam.. David Hey has provided a detailed account of the Hearth tax records for Lady Day in that year in his book 'The Hearth Tax Returns for South Yorkshire Lady Day 1672'.

Firstly though I must admit I knew nothing about the Hearth Tax until reading that book, so the following is a brief summary.

The tax was introduced in1671 following the Restoration of the monarchy in the person of Charles II and was introduced to help pay the expense of maintaining the Royal household. The tax was calculated on the number of hearths or chimneys a property had. The rate was 2 shillings a year per hearth, one shilling being due at Michaelmas (Sept 29th) and the other shilling payable on Lady Day (March 25th). Like most taxes of the sort it was unpopular as it was felt that an inspection of peoples' homes was intrusive. Some people blocked up hearths to avoid paying the tax. If discovered it seems the penalty was that they had to pay double. If you could persuade a minister, churchwarden or an Overseer of the Poor and two Justices of the Peace to certify that you were poor you would be exempt from paying the tax. Properties that had a very small rental value were also exempt.

The records for Upper Hallam show 86 properties were potentially taxable. They show just the names of the people liable but with one exception. For some reason Fullwood Hall is listed just as Fullwood Hall. It looks as though the compiler of the list may have thought this referred to a member of the Hall family with an unusual first name! It should have said George Fox.

Of the 86 properties upon which tax was payable by the person living in them, six have the word 'poore' written next to them. Those names were:-

John Lockwood

Widow Tillinson

Anne Stores

Alise Maskell

Thomas Justice

Widow Armitage

Each of the above are recorded as having just one hearth at their homes. One was by far the most common number. Over 50 had a single hearth and 15 had just two hearths. It seems smithy hearths were also included as the entries for John Dale, Philip Haxsworth and Rob Hinde all state they had 2 hearths including one in their smithy. Presumably these were blacksmiths who may also have been metalworking in local cutlery and penknife production, although there is no proof of this. The reason smithies were listed separately at this time is probably because the Cutlers Company were waging a vigorous campaign to have industrial hearths excluded from the tax. David Hey thinks the separate entries for smithies may be because it was uncertain as to whether tax was payable for these. Eventually they were exempted.

At the higher end of the social scale the entries record

John Machin	11 hearths
Robert Hall	8 hearths
Fullwood Hall	7 hearths
Henry Broomhead	5 hearths (including 3 at Scargill House)

Robert Hall certainly lived at Stumperlowe Hall but I have struggled to find John Machin's 11 hearth property. I thought Whirlow Hall or Whiteley Wood Hall were possibilities but these were both in the neighbouring Ecclesall Bierlow section so those can be excluded. The only others I can think of are Bennett Grange (probably then known as Birks Green) or possibly an Inn, as such establishments were hit hard by the tax because of having hearths for patrons in many rooms. The only inn I know of in the region was Water Carr Hall, near Carr Bridge, but it seems that was built some years after 1672.

The name Machin or Machon commonly occurs (particularly in the adjoining parish) but I have not been able to find anything about either John Machin or his property. Odd because on the face of it this must have been the grandest house in Upper Hallam at the time!

Following the hasty departure of King James II in 1688 and the accession of William III and his Stuart wife Queen Mary, the Hearth Tax was quickly abolished in 1689. Hallam's householders were not spared for long as in 1696 the more famous and longer lasting Window Tax was brought in, this time to offset the loss of revenue to the crown from the practice of clipping silver coins.

If the Hearth Tax was unpopular, the Window Tax was even more so. The flat rate was again 2 shillings a year per house with up to 10 windows. If you had between 10 and 20 windows you paid an extra 4 shillings a year. If you were unlucky enough to have more than 20 windows you had to pay an extra 8 shillings. In 1709 a top rate of 20 shillings was brought in for houses with over 30 windows. There were various changes in rates and methods of calculation over the years until the tax was abolished in 1851 following pressure from Doctors who argued that a lack of light was a significant cause of ill-health in their patients. To add insult to injury for the poor taxpayers of Hallam, a tax known as the House Tax was introduced at the same time in 1696 and was probably collected at the same time as the Window Tax. The combined taxes were imposed on the houses in Upper Hallam for well over 100 years as the House tax was only abolished in 1834

The earliest tax I know of to affect this area was the Geld. An Anglo-Saxon tax based on land ownership (usully 2 shillings per hide of land). It was originally brought in by the Saxons to pay off the Danes but was used 4 times by William I who also paid off the Norse/Danes after the conquest.

Moving forward a few centuries, there is a record in the Court Rolls of Willelmus du Hallun and Elena du Hallan paying the Poll tax in the year 1379. The Poll tax was payable by everyone regardless of income. It was levied on three separate occasions to meet expenses in connection with the wars in France. in 1377 the rate was 4 pennies (a groat). For those born after UK decimalization that is one third of a shilling, and a shilling was a twentieth of a pound, only it wasn't because they didn't have shillings or pound coins that early! A pound then was the equivalent of a pounds weight of silver and 240 pennies were of equivalent value to that pound. It seems the tax for 1379 was also 4 pennies, but the 1381 rate was a massive 12 pennies.

The tax did not survive beyond 1381 as it was a significant cause of the Peasants' Revolt. It seems that throughout the country people reacted badly as the poll returns for 1381 show a recorded population reduction of one third compared with the numbers for 1377. Whether this was tax avoidance or tax evasion I have no idea but a significant number of people seem to have managed to disappear from the official records in the four years between 1377 and 1381. Presumably Upper Hallam and Willemus and Elena were no exception to the general trend. The Black Death plague effect pre-dates both dates so that certainly was not the cause of population 'disappearance' in this case!

Upper Hallam was never well populated so will not have yielded much for the tax collectors. In 1672 there were 86 properties potentially liable to pay the Hearth Tax. Hunter reports that there were 105 houses in the township in 1796, an increase of less than 20 in over a hundred years. He states

'This population is rather dispersed over the township in single houses or in long straggling hamlets rather than collected in villages'

From the sources mentioned below I have put together the population figures for the early to mid19[th] century. It seems as though there was significant growth in people living in the area through the eighteenth century, a trend which continued into the following century.

Population figures for Upper Hallam 1801-1861

Year	Population
1801	794
1811	866
1821	1018
1831	1035
1841	1401
1851	1499
1861	1643

This is what the 1840 Parliamentary Gazetteer of England and Wales says of Upper Hallam:-

'A township in the parish of Sheffield, W Riding of Yorkshire. It lies three and a half miles WSW of Sheffield. There is an endowed daily school here.

Acres	*5,870*
Homes	*189*
Pop in 1801	*794*
In 1831	*1,035*
Poor Rates in 1838	*£498 and 1 shilling*

The great tract of Upper Hallam called Fulwood retains something of its' pristine forest character.'

It seems therefore that Fulwood was still largely wooded in 1840. The poor rates of well over two pounds per household would have been quite a burden on so few inhabitants. For many centuries since the Reformation, beginning with the Poor Law of 1572, each parish was responsible for its own poor and Trustees for administering relief were appointed.

In Upper Hallam, workhouse cottages were acquired by such Trustees to provide accommodation for the local poor.

Thirty years later in his Imperial Gazetteer of England and Wales of 1870-72 John Marius Wilson repeats much of the above information but adds that the Township was, by then, in the Ecclesall-Bierlow district, and that the hamlets were scattered with the 3.5 mile distance from Sheffield being an average distance.

Upper Hallam then had a Real Property (all land and buildings) value of £7,961 of which £10 related to mines and £140 was in respect of quarries. The mines would probably include the coal mines at Ringinglow and the quarries would include many of the small operations carried out at outlying farms like Brown Edge but also those much closer to modern development such as the quarry near the site of Fulwood chapel on Whiteley Lane.

The source also states that there were 338 houses in Upper Hallam and that steel working and cutlery making were carried on there. It also mentions a church (Christchurch in Fulwood) and an Independent chapel (Fulwood again) and also a Methodist chapel in Ranmoor .

There was a local dialect spoken in Upper Hallam comprising words used there '*among the rude and simple*' people living in that remote area, which words are '*not found and scarcely understood in the more populous parts,*' The following list of 'Hallamshire' words, commonly used in the period 1790-1810, described by the Rev Joseph Hunter in his book 'The Hallamshire Glossary' were probably as much used in Upper Hallam as in the rest of Hallamshire

Addle	to get or to earn
Booty	to play booty is to act deceptively
Clarty	dirty with a degree of stickiness
Cuttle-Headed	foolish
Dawkin	an idle slothful person
Dither	to shake with cold
Dizen	to dress one's self out with showy finery
Fatched	troubled, perplexed in mind, hurried with overmuch business
Jumps	short stays
Knock-Knobbler	the person who perambulates the church during divine service to keep order
Scrome	to walk or climb with long strides or awkwardly
Sleat	to encourage such as a dog to attack
Smittle	to Infect
Sprottle	to struggle with inefficacious vehemence

Taching-ends	remains of waxed thread begged of the shoemakers by schoolboys on which to string their cob-nuts
Toot	action of prying into anything a little more curiously than the person observed likes
Trapes	a very untidy wench
Unbethink	to recollect

I quite like the idea of being a knock-knobbler, but it would probably not be the best job for a cuttle-headed dawkin like me- I'd end up fetched.

No doubt our poor tax collector suffered people sleating their dogs on him while he was tooting.

Apparently those living in Upper Hallam shared their dialect and manners more closely with those in the Peak district of Derbyshire than with their closer Sheffield neighbours. In his book 'Hallamshire The History and Topography of the Parish of Sheffield' Reverend Hunter observes that

This is the more remarkable since they are cut off from their neighbours on that side {The Peak} by long tracts of high moorland which till lately were crossed only by narrow bridleways, along which was raised, at intervals, a rude stone pillar or a wooden pole while scarcely a winter passed which did not prove them to be insufficient to guide the belated traveller on his way. One of these, called Stanedge pole is still remaining, which serves the further purpose of marking the divisions of the counties of York and Derby at which meet the three parishes of Hathersage, Ecclesfield and Sheffield.

Almost 200 years since those words were written Stanedge Pole is still there marking the county boundary. The pole itself has been replaced many times but is still an important landmark that people feel is worth preserving.
Here it is. The base is made of metal these days but is still a prominent landmark. The road leading up to it is part of The Long Causeway, a medieval trading route over to Hathersage and beyond.

Fig 25 Stanedge Pole
A Sunday afternoon walk along the Long Causeway to Stanedge Pole and beyond to Stanedge Edge. A pole has been in this position since at least 1550. The present pole is the trunk of a locally felled larch tree

CHAPTER 10

THE TROTTERS AND RINGINGLOW

Robert Trotter's early life had nothing whatsoever to do with Fulwood, Sheffield, or even South Yorkshire. He was born in Berwick on Tweed, then part of Scotland, in 1759, and spent most of his childhood with his parents who brought him to Durham to work in a corn mill until they rather carelessly allowed him to be abducted by a group of miners from Barnsley. I do not know if this was common mining recruiting practice, but it does seem to have a lot in common with the way Royal Navy recruits were press-ganged into service at that time. His employers, being from Barnsley, are however, unlikely to have offered him a King's shilling for his services.

It seems he did not enjoy life in the Barnsley coalfield too much for he deserted his employers and found his way to Ringinglow where he obtained work on Marsh Green Farm. He does not seem to have entirely escaped his past life there though, as he was involved in sinking the first pit in Ringinglow near what is now Ringinglow Road.

He seems to have done well for he married a local girl Sarah Walker in Sheffield Cathedral on 14th December 1784 and started a mine of his own in Ringinglow. This mine was given the glorious name of the Deep Sick Mine and was on waste or Common Land of the local manor. At first he paid nothing for use of the land but once it came to the Duke of Rutland's agents' attention that the mine seemed profitable he was charged 5 shillings a year rent. This was increased to three guimeas (£3 and 3 shillings) a year payable by his widow and son George who continued to operate the mine after Robert's death in 1827.

Robert originally lived in one of the Carr Houses on Quiet Lane (see also the section about George Fox) and he built what was essentially a shed at Ringinglow in which to store mined coal and his tools. Unfortunately it seems that certain locals were wont to help themselves to coal from this shed, as well as his tools, so Robert decided to '*add another storey lengthwise*' and go and live there with his family. This house acquired the ironic title locally of Moorcock Hall. George built a further extension lengthwise and lived there until his death in 1859. A further Trotter, Hiriam Trotter, the great grandson of Robert lived there until 1892. In 1911 it was pulled down and rebuilt to provide a home renamed 'Moorcot (now Moor Cottage) for the once landlord of the Norfolk Arms, a Mr Priest.

Much of the above, and the following information, comes from Muriel Hall's books 'The Mayfield Valley' and 'More of Mayfield Valley with Old Fulwood'. She also speaks of Ringinglow Wire Mill so, while we are in Ringinglow we may as well call into the Norfolk Arms, castellated in 1803 to match the decoration of the Round House, for refreshment and, on the way in, look at the row of terrace cottages built on the same side of the road at the junction with Fulwood Lane.

Six of these cottages were built to house the Wire Mill workers and two others were added later. The Wire Mill itself was directly behind these houses. Herbert Trotter writes in the Clarion Ramblers Handbook (1950/1 edition) that it was built in 1844. It seems they originally took coal from local drift workings a few hundred yards away until a fire had burned down the Mill in 1867. Shortly before this event someone had the idea that the coal seam seemed to be pointing in the direction of the mill and that if they dug down deep enough they would find their own coal.

A shaft was sunk in the Mill Yard. At a depth of 196 feet they found the coal. It seems the Trotter family were heavily involved. Joe Trotter and Sam Millward were colliers and a Hiriam Trotter (though not the one who lived at Moorcock Hall) was the engineman. As was often the case with mines, water ingress made the operation dangerous and the Authorities ordered closure of the entrance in 1901.

The fire at the Mill seems to have started during a dispute between the owner and the workers. The owner refused to pay the going rate to the workers who went on strike. The managers and apprentices continued to work. It seems the building was insured for £1,000 only a month before the fire and this sum seems to have been paid out on the assumption that the fire must have been caused by the strikers. In these more cynical times it would not be hard to come up with another possible reason!

The mill chimney stood for some time after abandonment until it was pulled down in 1912. The lightning conductor was taken by Herbert Trotter who '*made toastin forks for nearly ivverybody at Fulwood*' according to the Clarion Rambler correspondent also named Herbert Trotter.

There is apparently a sough that drained the mine which empties into the Porter valley at a place called Hell Bank but I am not sufficiently obsessed to seek it out. Before leaving Ringinglow though, the oddest bulding still standing is the octagonal 'round' house opposite the Norfolk Arms. It was built sometime between 1758 and 1760 as a Toll House on a crossroads on the Sheffield to Chapel-on-the-Frith road but its' working life ended by 1825 when the roads were demoted to Parish Highways. On the other side of what was Houndkirk Road from the toll house was an old weighbridge. This is marked as 'site of' on a plan to a sale of the Norfolk Arms Estate in 1896 a copy of which is reproduced overleaf

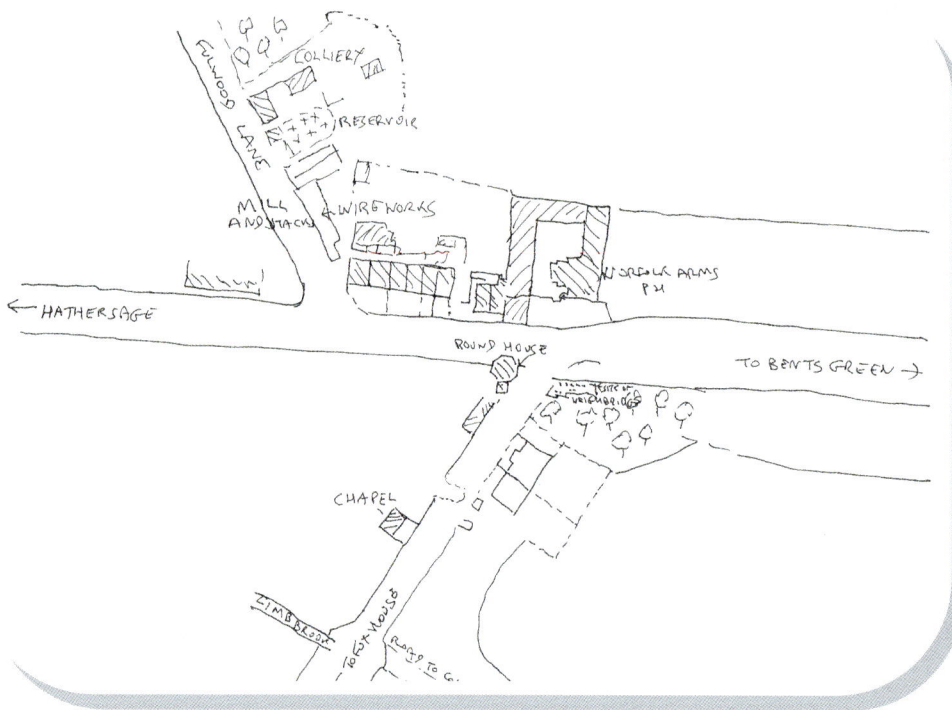

The Ringinglow Inn (now the Norfolk Arms) must have had plenty of custom from the various industrial operations being carried on next door and in the neighbourhood. The plan shows just a few of them!

Fig 26 Ringinglow 1896 Sale plan extract (with annotations)

The chapel shown was built in 1864 but was never well attended. It is now a private house. In 1886, when the chapel was operative, a small shop and larder existed, operating from a single-storied outbuilding by the Round House. It seems it remained open until the early 1940's. Apparently, in the late 19th Century, a pony and trap operated from another outbuilding to take people on 'excursions' to Sheffield for provisions.

The heyday for the toll house came in the year 1797/8 when toll receipts were £421. This was the second highest receipt for all the toll bars in Sheffield for that year. This shows how busy the place must have been. The only higher toll take for that year was from the toll at Handsworth!

Fig 27
The Round House

A small industrial railway also ran between Furnace Farm and Copperas Farm. These days Ringinglow has no more heavy industry (The Mayfield Alpacas on Fulwood Lane do not count) Although a Neolithic stone axe and a flint knife were found in 1952 near Fulwood Lane, it is thought unlikely that they were hunting Alpaca.in Ringinglow at the time!

CHAPTER 11

PATRICK DANIEL AND FULWOOD COTTAGE HOMES

A little over a hundred years ago, back in 1902, the Ecclesall Board of Guardians decided that neither the workhouse nor the various small homes they already had, were satisfactory places for the children in their care. They were to acquire additional responsibilities as they were taking over administration of what was previously Upper Hallam on 1st April 1904 and so land was therefore acquired in Fulwood and a local firm of Architects were approached to design several, substantial, semi-detached properties in which to house the children. The firm were well used to designing public buildings as they had been consulted in connection with several Sheffield Board schools. The name of the firm may sound familiar, although in a somewhat different context - Holmes and Watson. At least the schools they designed weren't elementary.

Fulwood Cottage Homes were built together with a house for the master and his wife (invariably a matron) to look after the children in their care. The foundation stone was laid by the chairman of the Guardians, William Aldam Milner, who is commemorated on a stone set into the substantial superintendent's house near the entrance to the site off Blackbrook Road in Fulwood, now known as 'Moorside', where it celebrates the date of October 9th 1903.

Fig 28
Fulwood Cottage Homes from the south. The porches and garages were not part of the original construction

It was an exposed, remote and airy site. The 1905 OS map shows the 22 acre site in splendid isolation with the entire area between Blackbrook Road and Crimicar Lane being fields. Indeed the nearby Lodge Moor area was chosen as sites for the isolation hospitals at Lodge Moor and Crimicar Lane. A First World War army training camp was also established at nearby Redmires, to replicate the grim conditions in Flanders . The above photograph gives some indication of the isolation of the site.

The houses were laid out to make the most of the fact that the site was south-facing. Normally this type of development was in the form of a circle around a central green space but these cottage homes were set out as two parallel, south-facing rows to maximize sunlight, a large green filling the central space. Near the entrance stood a lodge (now demolished) and the Master's house with outbuildings behind. To the north was the boys' workshop and, to the south, the girls' equivalent. On the side furthest from the Blackbrook Road entrance an isolation house for the sick was also built.

78 children were initially transferred to the homes, beginning on 30th September 1905 Eventually the complex could take 240 children once all of the houses were built. Each 'semi' had a house-mother, with a bedroom to herself, and two bedroom dormitories one with room for 6 girls and one for 6 boys. Food was cooked in the house kitchen and eaten around a large table there. It seems that later the houses accommodated single sex occupants, the girls to the south and the boys to the north.

In 1912/3 an Assembly Hall was added together with the prominent Water Tower which took a water supply from the nearby conduit. A laundry and other houses were also built. At some point the dormitories were expanded to each take 7 children so each semi then housed 14 children and the house mother. Clothing and feeding that many must have been something of a challenge and, no doubt, the children were given their own tasks to help ensure all were clothed and fed. The boys certainly were set to planting and harvesting vegetables in the central green. The local studies library has a photo of them hard at work. The girls, helped with the mending and making of clothes in the sewing room

Many of the children went to school locally. The school they were sent to in the early days was housed in the building that later became the 'Mayfield Centre 'but was then the Mayfield Valley School which had been built in around 1875 and was a Board school. Unusually there was also an adjoining master's house because of the 'remote' location. In 1876 there were 76 children taught there, but by 1906, when the Cottage Homes opened, they needed to build an extra classroom and, by 1912, there were 113 children from the Homes and another 72 'locals'. It seems as though children came from as far away as Redmires and Houndkirk Farm (beyond Ringinglow) to attend the school. In later years, when mechanical transport became more available, the Cottage Home children were taken by bus to schools all over Sheffield.

The school records indicate the Cottage Home children's attendance was erratic due to outbreaks of Measles, Chicken Pox, Scarlet Fever and Mumps, each of which meant that the Cottage Homes children were confined to the Homes. At harvest and haymaking the local farmers children were away helping their relatives and bad weather sometimes prevented attendance. In the last week of January 1940 it is reported that no children attended on the Monday and Tuesday, one managed to get in on Thursday and two attended on Wednesday and Friday!

Not all children stayed in the homes for the rest of their childhood. Some returned back to their families, but orphans and those without the opportunity of returning to their families were given training to equip them for adult life. As already mentioned, there was a workshop for the boys where they learned tailoring and shoemaking in an upstairs room, above a store room, while the girls were trained in their upstairs room, in a separate house, in sewing and knitting where they made clothes and black stockings. Under the Water Tower there were carpentry and painting workshops. There was also a nursery as some of the children taken in were only babies.

On 1st April 1930 operation of the homes was taken over by Sheffield Corporation. The people in charge at the homes remained, Lionel and Freda Hildreth. With improved transport facilities, the children were able to go away to the coast on annual holidays . There is a photo of over two hundred of them crowding Sheffield Station.They were bought new clothes for such outings. The boys also had their own brass band that would tour the grounds playing carols on Christmas Day. There may be a sad twist to this tale though.

The homes continued to operate until 1960, after which they became what is known locally as 'the Naughty Girls' Homes or, to give it its' Sunday name, Moorside Approved School for Senior Girls (for which use it was approved on 1st April 1960). It housed up to 84 girls between the ages of 15 and 17. Thereafter it was used as a temporary home for the Vietnamese Boat people refugees in the early 1980's prior to their resettlement. There then followed a period of abandonment until a national firm of housebuilders acquired the site and converted the houses into private dwellings. Under the builders' decorations indelicate messages can sometimes still be found scrawled on the walls, or in cupboards, possibly left by the 'naughty girls.' I am told quite a few tradesmen would go no further than the gates for fear of what might await them within. Photographs show a chapel, shop, canteen and rest room and the girls wore typical 60's clothing

Children grew up and found employment. Some worked on local farms, some in the armed forces and some in service. Cottage Home girls were apparently 'much sought after' in Fulwood and Ranmoor as serving girls in the days when those still existed. Much of the above information has been supplied by Marjorie Dunn whose booklet ' For the Love of Children' is an excellent source of much interesting information on the cottage homes and the poor children of Sheffield.

Several of the children from the homes fought in the two world wars. The plaque commemorating them is at Kelham Island Museum and a transcription of the names is available in the Sheffield Archives.
In the 1914 European War of Honour 5 boys are described as entering service with the Royal Navy and 34 with 'land forces.' Marjorie Dunn's book shows a photograph of boys in uniform from Blyth Nautical College. It seems that the then Superintendent, Mr Deacon, encouraged the boys to join the forces in preference to going down the mines to work. No doubt though, mining, or working in the steel mills, would have been the fate of many of the boys.

The numbers listed for the 1939-45 war are astonishing. The following table shows the number of individuals from the Cottage Homes who joined up with the various branches of the armed forces. This time girls are also mentioned

55	Navy
3	Royal Marines
10	Merchant Navy
3	WRNS
149	Army
26	ATS girls
9	WAAF
32	RAF

287	Total of those enlisted for WWII

Sadly, ,there are 13 names duplicated. The inscription reads:-

'Greater love hath no man than that a man lay down his life for his friends ' John c15 v13.

It seems as though these were casualties during the war. Pat Daniel, one of the three marines, was one such named. I have researched the name and it seems that his full name was Patrick Gordon Reuben Daniel who was born in early 1928. His mother's maiden name was Clarke and she was from Ecclesall Bierlow (the parish in which the homes were situated at that time.) His name does not appear in the list of those admitted to the homes in the years 1928 to 1935 so he must have been admitted sometime after 1935. It is likely that he was one of those boys that played in the brass band at the homes as he joined the band of the Royal Marines. His death is recorded on 12th May 1943 and he is interred at Douglas Cemetery in the Isle of Man. He was only 15 when he died. It seems the Isle of Man was quite a dangerous place for those in the services during the war years. No less than 142 British war graves are on the island. These are from the navy, the army, the RAF, the merchant navy and one described as 'miscellaneous'. Maybe that is our bandsman. It seems that of all the branches of the forces in the war the highest percentage casualty rate was for bandsman. Patrick's death certificate gives the following additional information

His address is given as 50 Northfield Road Crookes and his occupation was Band Boy RMB x2012 attached to the Royal Navy School of Music at Howstrake, Corchan. His place of death is given as Lagabury Gully, Conchan, Isle of Man, which gives a clue as to the cause of death.

'Fracture of the skull then and their sustained by misadventure when climbing on the cliffs in search of gulls' eggs.'

A very sad end to such a short life.

The plaque commemorating him together with his comrades was originally housed in the Assembly Hall and had been presented to the superintendent by a former child resident. The assembly Hall is shown on the plan and photograph below.

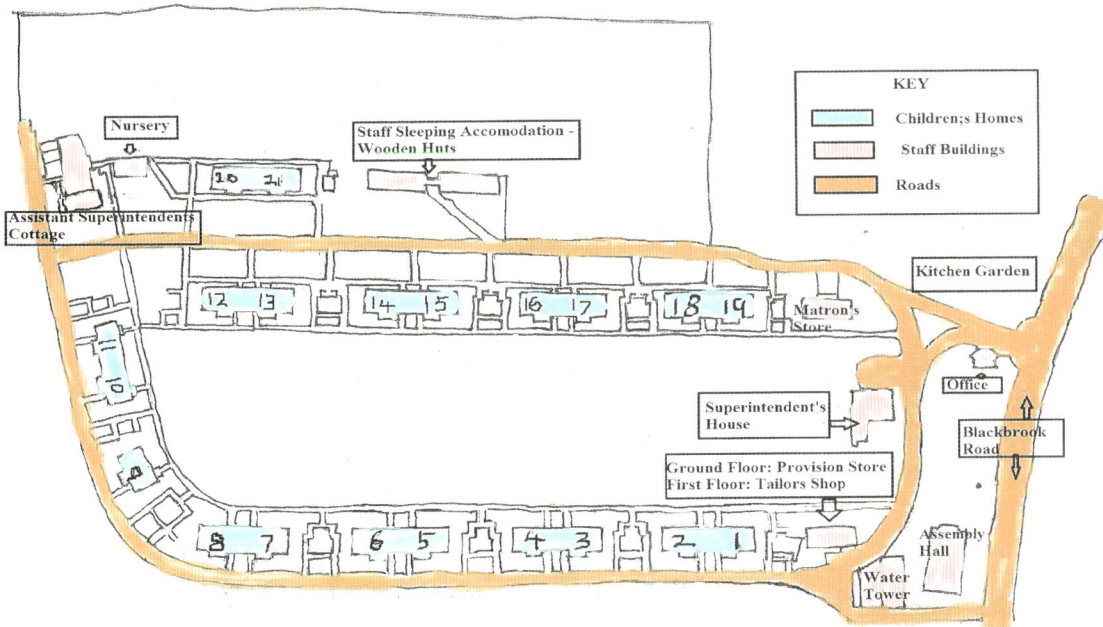

Fig 29 1953 Plan of Moorside Cottage Homes with original house numbers

Fig 30
The Water Tower (right) and Assembly
Hall (left) built in 1912/3

It seems as though many children made close friendships in the homes and reunions were organised from time to time. Of course, not all the children were happy there. Some ran away and were punished. Those that return to the site of their childhood have wildly different reactions. Some look on the houses with something like affection, others with dread. Some delivery drivers who lived in the homes during their own childhood certainly want to get out as quickly as possible. Now and then people stand in the road just looking ………………………………..

CHAPTER 11

<u>ELSIE MURDOCH AND LODGE MOOR HOSPITAL</u>

It was not feeling very Christmassy at Lodge Moor although it was well into December. The temperatures hadn't dropped below freezing all month. It was 1955 and the country was beginning to emerge from the rationing days of the war. Despite the heavy bombing in the industrial areas, the bombs had left the far West of Sheffield untouched. It was Friday evening. People were about to return home from work and their thoughts were drifting towards Christmas shopping, what was on at the cinema that weekend, whether to drop in at the Sportsman or the Three Merry Lads, even whether Wednesday would win tomorrow. All the usual thoughts at going home time on a Friday evening.

Lodge Moor Hospital had started life in 1888. It had been built with a workforce of 300 who managed to construct 12 temporary wooden wards within two months to contain those suffering from the Smallpox outbreak in Sheffield in the years 1887/8. Stone built wards had followed, and the iconic tower visible for miles around had been built in 1905. The hospital had greatly expanded over the years and had coped with Scarlet Fever, Diphtheria, Typhoid and even the 1918 lethal influenza that had hit Sheffield (and much of Western Europe) at the end of the first world war. The nearby army camp at Redmires had been pressed into service to cope with another serious smallpox outbreak in 1925, and very recently the hospital had started to take paraplegics. Only the previous year a spinal injuries unit had become established to help cope with the growing number of motor vehicle, pit and factory accidents.

On 10th December, a young nurse who was a patient, recovering on one of the wards at the hospital, fancied a cup of tea, mostly to relieve the boredom. She was in an individual cubicle . There were many things she would rather be doing than sitting alone in bed on a Friday night and a few minutes making a brew would help pass the time.

Doctor Joseph Kennedy, the Medical Superintendent, was sitting in his office, working on a Friday evening. It was raining and he was glad to be indoors. A couple of hospital orderlies were helping clear away the tea things on a ward.

Many miles away, over the Irish Sea, a young American pilot with a striking resemblance to Elvis Presley, was flying his aircraft, a Thunderstreak F.84 over the Irish Sea. The whole fleet of those aircraft had been grounded earlier in the year after a large number had suffered engine failures when flying in heavy rain or snow. They were all back in the air now, and although it was December he was thinking all was OK now. He had taken off from his base at Sculthorpe in Norfolk for instrument training earlier that day. A short time later, Selwyn Williams, picked up the telephone at his home in Lodge Moor Lane and was making a call, the 19 year old patient was waiting for her tea to brew, the superintendent and the orderlies were carrying on with their work as normal. Up in the air though, all was not so calm.

The pilot knew something was wrong and had headed for home. It was misty and raining and he couldn't land at the Isle of Man. The lifeboat had earlier been called out into the Irish Sea when it appeared to observers that he was in trouble. Faint radio contact from him was picked up at the American Air Force control tower at Bartonwood in Lancashire as he flew over Derbyshire. He could not hear them so he was on his own.

The pilot had little choice. His engine had suffered a flame out and had died. He had tried to restart it without success. It had reached the point where he had to get out. He was at around 3,500 feet and losing height. If he left it much longer he was unlikely to survive even with a parachute. He bailed out, but survived. He damaged his ankle but was picked up near Hathersage.

The hospital had no warning. The plane was dropping silently from the cloudy skies. Mr Williams was still on the phone, the patient was drinking her tea, the hospital staff were still working away , when the aircraft crashed into the hospital at an estimated speed of 300 miles an hour. One of the orderlies on the ward describes it like this:-

'There was a tremendous crash. A gaping hole appeared in one corner of the room and one of the wheels whizzed past me. It missed me by inches.'

The young patient could only look on in horror as her cubicle had disappeared in the path of devastation. The plane crashed through the North Ward where there were 12 patients in cubicles, many of whom were trapped under collapsing walls as the ceiling was stripped away by the plane. A corridor was demolished and a 14 cubicle ward also damaged before the plane came to rest near the ambulance station and the mortuary.

Dr Kennedy heard the crash and thought the tower had been hit. He ran outside and saw that the plane had come down about 50 yards from his office. The wreckage was on fire and ammunition stored in the wings was exploding. One of the orderlies was crawling, fire extinguisher in hand to help in the patient rescue efforts.

Mr Williams finished his call abruptly when he heard the crash. He dialled 999, and sped to the site in his car. He reported the following to 'the Times' where it was described the following morning:

'The single aircraft had crashed through the roof of a single storey building and sliced through three cubicles before hitting the ground. The tail was leaning against the walls. A number of people with blackened faces were running about. The wreckage was blazing fiercely.'

As news of the disaster spread, off-duty staff rushed to the site to help with the rescue effort. They were later commended by Councillor Worrall, the Chairman of the Hospital Committee, for '*risking their own safety from bullets, flying debris and fire*'. They managed to get all the patients out. There were 8 injured, three children and five adults. None of the children were seriously hurt and two of the adults suffered shock but no other physical injury. Two adults suffered minor injuries but one, Elsie Murdoch was unlucky enough to have been in one of the cubicles that suffered a direct hit. She was retrieved from the wreckage alive but sadly she died shortly afterwards in the company of one of the nurses at the hospital.

Elsie was only 46. She was married, lived in Walkley and was the mother of 5 children. She was due to be discharged on the Monday morning following the weekend. Her photograph appeared on the front page of the Star on Saturday 10th December 1955 (see overleaf) and the crash was reported in the Times and was also the headline article in the Daily Mirror that day.

The hospital closed to patients in the 1990's and, like the two schools and Fulwood Cottage homes has been converted into residential development. The information above comes from the various reports in the Times, the Daily Mirror and the Morning Telegraph. For those too young to remember, the last was essentially, a morning edition of the Star which itself used to come out in the afternoon!

A far more detailed and readable account of the crash (with photos) is to be found on Chris Hobbs' website at http://www.chrishobbs.com/lodgemoor1955.htm.

Fig 31

The Lodge Moor Hospital former lodge and entrance with the tower in the background

Fig 32 The accident as reported on the front page of the Sheffield Star of 10th December 1955
Reproduced with their kind permission

I hope you have found at least something of interest in the rather eclectic mix of stories contained in this collection. If not you can at least be comforted by the knowledge that all money I receive from sales is to go to non magpie-related charities.

SOURCES and FURTHER READING

Books

John Austen	Historical Notes on Old Sheffield Druggists	1961
David Bentley	The Sheffield Hanged 1750-1864	2002
Roy Davey	Reminiscing around Rivelin	2005
Michael Dyson	The Roman Diploma of AD 124	2017
Marjorie Dunn	For the Love of Children.	c1990
Shirley Frost	Whirlow The Story of an Ancient Sheffield Hamlet	1990
Ivor Gatty	Fulwood Spa Essay (Sheffield Archives)	1943
Muriel Hall	The Mayfield Valley	1972
Muriel Hall	More of the Mayfield Valley	1974
David Hey	A History of Sheffield	2010 Ed
David Hey	A History of the South Yorkshire Countryside	2015
David Hey	The Hearth Tax Returns for South Yorkshire Lady Day 1672	1991
Rev Joseph Hunter	Hallamshire: The History and Topography of the Parish of Sheffield in the County of York	1819
Rev Joseph Hunter	The Hallamshire Glossary	1829
Elizabeth Perkins	A Tree in the Valley	1982
David Price	Sheffield Troublemakers Rebels and Radicals in Sheffield History	2012
Roger Redfern	Fulwood and the Mayfield Valley	2005
Thomas Short	The Natural Experimental and Medicinal History of the Mineral Waters of Derbyshire Lincolnshire and Yorkshire	1734
Thomas Short	The Mineral Waters of England Vol 2	1740
Howard Smith	The Long Causeway	2017
J Edward Vickers	The Ancient Suburbs of Sheffield	1971
Peter Warr	The Growth of Ranmoor, Hangingwater and Nether Green	2009

Websites for more information

http://archaeologicalservices.com/projects/whirlow-hall-farm
http://chrishobbs.com/lodgemoor1955.htm
http://www.domesdaybook.co.uk
http://www.thetimetravellers.org.uk/
http://www.ourbroomhall.org.uk/content/explore/topics/politics/the-broom-hall-riots

Periodicals

The Gentlemans Magazine vol 100
The Star Dec 10th 1955

Documents

Copy will of John Fox	Sheffield Archives
1828 Petition	Original in Sheffield Archives